EXPOSED

ALSO BY MARK SCHAPIRO
Circle of Poison: Pesticides and People in a Hungry World
(co-authored with David Weir)

EXPOSED

The Toxic Chemistry
of Everyday Products
and
What's at Stake
for American Power

MARK SCHAPIRO

CHELSEA GREEN PUBLISHING
WHITE RIVER JUNCTION, VERMONT

Developmental Editor: John Barstow
Project Manager: Emily Foote
Copy Editor: Cannon Labrie
Proofreader: Robin Model-Lornitzo
Designer: Peter Holm

Printed in the United States
First printing, July 2007
10 9 8 7 6 5 4 3   09 10 11 12 13

Chelsea Green Publishing Company
Post Office Box 428
White River Junction, VT 05001
(802) 295-6300
www.chelseagreen.com

The Chelsea Green Publishing Company is committed
to preserving ancient forests and natural resources. We
elected to print this title on 30% postconsumer recycled
paper, processed chlorine-free. As a result, for this printing,
we have saved:

18 Trees (40' tall and 6-8" diameter)
6,494 Gallons of Wastewater
12 million BTUs Total Energy
834 Pounds of Solid Waste
1,565 Pounds of Greenhouse Gases

Chelsea Green Publishing made this paper choice because
we and our printer, Thomson-Shore, Inc., are members
of the Green Press Initiative, a nonprofit program dedi-
cated to supporting authors, publishers, and suppliers
in their efforts to reduce their use of fiber obtained
from endangered forests. For more information, visit:
www.greenpressinitiative.org.

Environmental impact estimates were made using the Environmental Defense Paper Calculator.
For more information visit: www.papercalculator.org.

Library of Congress Cataloging-in-Publication Data
Schapiro, Mark, 1955-
  Exposed : the toxic chemistry of everyday products and what's at stake for American power / Mark
Schapiro.
     p. cm.
  Includes index.
  ISBN 978-1-933392-15-8 (hardcover) — ISBN 978-1-60358-058-8 (pbk.)
  1. Industries—Environmental aspects—United States. 2. Business enterprises—Environmental
aspects—United States. 3. Green technology—Government policy—Europe. 4. Competition—
Environmental aspects—United States. 5. Environmental policy—United States. I. Title. II. Title:
Toxic chemistry of everyday products.

  HC110.E5S386 2007
  363.17—dc22
                                    2007019982

Our Commitment to Green Publishing
Chelsea Green sees publishing as a tool for cultural change and ecological stewardship. We strive to align
our book manufacturing practices with our editorial mission and to reduce the impact of our business
enterprise on the environment. We print our books and catalogs on chlorine-free recycled paper, using
soy-based inks whenever possible. This book may cost slightly more because we use recycled paper, and
we hope you'll agree that it's worth it. Chelsea Green is a member of the Green Press Initiative
(www.greenpressinitiative.org), a nonprofit coalition of publishers, manufacturers, and authors working to
protect the world's endangered forests and conserve natural resources.
  Exposed was printed on Natures Natural, a 30 percent post-consumer-waste recycled, old-growth-forest-
free paper supplied by Thomson-Shore.

For Shawn and Lorraine Schapiro,
who would have understood,
and for Deborah, who continues to.

CONTENTS

Introduction

The year 2008 unfolded like a tragi-comedy as the distance grew ever wider between the Bush administration's ideological conceits and reality. Long-held presumptions were toppled from what turns out to have been a very shaky pedestal.

Masters of the free market? The crash of 2008 took that pretense off the table. Deregulation as the means for ensuring prosperity and economic growth? Gone, with the rising acknowledgement that government's retreat from oversight over the excesses of the market gave rise to an epidemic of just such excesses.

Number one in the global economy? No longer: Wall Street's fiascos, the surge of developing economies, and the increasing assertiveness of the European Union—now the world's largest single market—have displaced U.S. dominance with multiple poles of global power.

The season of collapsing paradigms continues as we face an environmental crisis that is as loaded with unforeseen consequences as the economic crisis that shook the foundations of the global financial system. The signals of that crisis may be more diffuse—from fracturing eco-systems to rising rates of environmentally caused disease to accelerating climate change—but they have the same potential to deeply unsettle the status quo. Our bodies are registering the toxic effects of the chemical age and the planet is registering the heat from more than a century of rampant fossil energy use. Like the financial collapse, they demand concerted global action.

In place of solutions, however, Americans were offered a bluff. Promoted to the extreme by Bush but with bipartisan nurturing along the way over the past two decades, Americans have been told repeatedly that economic growth is incompatible with environmental progress.

But while the Bush administration retreated, the rest of the world did not wait; that bluff is being called. This book began when several years ago I began asking a question: What happens during this time of global interdependence when an economy comparable to America's in size and sophistication applies a different set of principles for protecting our environmental health than those that have long reigned in the United States?

For the first time in history, we now have a test case—the 27 countries and 495 million people that make up the European Union—to assess how an alternative strategy might work. And we have a control group—the United States, whose leaders clung to the status quo while the EU moved forward with an economic growth plan which places sustainability alongside competitiveness. Striking that balance continues to be a source of great contention in Europe, but it has already made the EU the world's leader in environmental protection. One result: Americans are now subject to an array of environmental hazards—revealed in these pages—from which others around the world are being protected.

Over the last five years, the EU has banned scores of toxic chemicals from use in an array of consumer goods; demanded higher rates of recyclability in the essential building blocks of electronics, automobiles, and other products; imposed stringent standards on energy usage; and required toxicity data on tens of thousands of chemicals never assessed for their safety in the United States. Many of these ideas were born in the U.S.A. but were nurtured, implemented, and expanded upon in Europe.

This book is an investigation into the multiple implications of that shift in global environmental power and into the economic effects of those initiatives. U.S. industry and its allies in the Bush administration initiated an unprecedented lobbying campaign to try to stop the

Europeans, arguing that their actions would hinder global trade, hamper innovation, and harm European competitiveness. What happened? Since first writing this book, further evidence suggests that protecting people's health, and the health of the environment, is good economics.

In 2007, after many of those European initiatives took effect, the growth rate in the GDP of the 15 core EU members was twenty percent higher than that of the United States—and, not incidentally, as the financial crisis of 2008 hit, the EU's rate of contraction was significantly slower than that of the U.S.

From Europe's biggest chemical companies to its single-product boutiques, new technologies are providing jobs and presenting a competitive challenge to U.S. companies across the world. A 2007 assessment by the Directorate General for the Environment, the EU's equivalent of the EPA, found that the "main impact" of the reforms has been "to shift resources from polluting sectors to more environmentally friendly sectors." Areas of job growth include pollution control, sustainable energy technologies, waste management, recycling and eco-tourism.

The Europeans are challenging another long-running American dogma—that regulation hampers innovation. In Germany, Europe's industrial powerhouse, the conservative government's Federal Environment Agency concluded in late 2007 that it was precisely Europe's new generation of environmental mandates which prompted industries across the continent to develop greener products—a market which is forecast to grow dramatically over the coming decades. The agency surveyed top executives at ninety European corporations and summarized their unambiguous conclusion: It was government prompting that was needed "to drive environmental innovation onward." Such measures were raising all companies to a new level playing field, while creating economies of scale to help ensure that fresh innovations could reach the market.

Nor are the effects of these initiatives limited to Europe; they are radiating through the global economy. As I discovered since this book was first published, state governments and the U.S. Congress have found themselves increasingly looking to Europe for guidance on how to approach our environmental challenges. Meanwhile, American companies are finding themselves compelled to abide by standards that they have long opposed in the United States in order to maintain access to the European market.

In the waning days of 2008, for example, U.S. chemical and manufacturing firms began meeting a new requirement to supply toxicity data for thousands of chemicals in their products in order to comply with the demands of an initiative launched not in Washington, DC, but in Brussels, capital of the EU. The initiative, called REACH — for Registration, Authorization and Evaluation of Chemicals — aims to remove from circulation the most toxic substances. First step: Collect the data. As of December 2008, half of the companies that submitted chemicals for registration with the European Chemical Agency came from outside Europe; most of those were either Chinese or American.

Now every U.S. exporter to Europe — there are thousands — must demonstrate the scientific back-up to their safety claims for products containing toxic chemicals, a move they have long and strenuously opposed in the United States. Are they carcinogens? Endocrine disrupters? Do they cause damage to the reproductive system or mutations in human genes? Are their potential dangers too great to permit them to remain in circulation? The U.S. Environmental Protection Agency does not have the power to demand the data to ask those questions, or to act on answers that are being supplied by independent scientists across the United States and around the world.

Into this new era of crumbling paradigms comes Barack Obama, assuming the presidency of a country that occupies a very different place than it did just a few years ago, not only in the world but in our own imagination. The ground is shifting under our feet. Uncertainty and its corollary, possibility, reigns. Obama may be uniquely suited to this new world of many players—in which the United States no longer acts alone. And as we all enter this shifting international terrain, this book suggests that there is something to be learned from that other major power across the Atlantic which has been facing the environmental challenges of the 21st century rather than walking away from them.

DECEMBER 8, 2008

1

Soft Power, Hard Edge

One afternoon in early 2006, I sat with fifty nervous engineers while they listened to a colleague explain how the foundations of the world economy were shifting beneath their feet. We were in a boxy conference room in the California town of Santa Clara. Some of the world's most recognizable products start their journey into the marketplace from this suburban hamlet, still young enough that the tar shines on the avenues. Companies like Dell, Apple, Sun, Intel, and many other lesser-known brands are headquartered nearby, together representing hundreds of billions of dollars in high-tech electronics sales across the world.

Most of the participants were senior engineers. It's fair to say that their fingerprints, or those of their colleagues, are somewhere inside the workings of your computer, your DVD player, your video-game consoles, or any number of dozens of other consumer and medical electronic devices. They are the brains behind many of the crown jewels of American ingenuity and entrepreneurship.

The meeting was held inside a conference room of Quanta Labs, which does reliability tests on new products that come out of these enterprises, subjecting them to stress tests—repeated exposure to water, heat, and fog, and to violent vibrations from a metal pillar intended to simulate an earthquake. Behind us, in a sealed room behind two-foot-thick concrete walls, a one-hundred-pound slab of steel hung from the roof, ready to pound any new product placed underneath it, to test how much abuse it could take over the sped-up course of a mechanical lifetime. Recently, they'd tested the cones in a nuclear reactor. As we met, that huge anvil, housed in a bulky steel cylinder, hung ready to drop.[1]

But the sword of Damocles hanging over the engineers' heads that day was not made of steel. It came, rather, from Europe. Three years earlier, the European Union had passed a series of directives to address the rising problems associated with electrical waste.

The European Commission estimates that each European citizen produces 3.3 tons of e-waste over the course of an average lifetime, trash that piles up in landfills and leeches toxins into the earth and water.[2] That waste comes from discarded computers, cell-phones, DVD players, toasters, refrigerators, clock radios, medical devices— most everything powered by electricity. Every engineer in the room was now being required to rethink the ingredients that enable their complex networks of circuits and chips to work. The Europeans had banned six of those substances—mercury, cadmium, lead, chromium, and two chemical flame retardants called polybromi- nated biphenyl flame retardants—from all electrically powered devices. These heavy metals and chemicals have been integral to the circuitry, solder, and casing of thousands of small and large electronic devices. The EU's initiative governing the toxics in electronics carried a bureaucratic title with an awkward acronym: the directive "on the restriction of the use of certain hazardous substances in electrical and electronic equipment," or RoHS. But that bland acronym was striking fear in the hearts of U.S. engineers and executives. The RoHS direc- tive became law after hundreds of studies suggested the ingredients could have potent carcinogenic and endocrine-disrupting effects. The EU also wanted to see its electronics recycled—and none of those six substances are recyclable. They are too toxic. These directives were changing the way business was conducted in Europe, and in the process threatening U.S. firms that failed to adapt with huge financial losses and waning global stature.

The U.S. Environmental Protection Agency had also conducted numerous studies on these same substances, as have many other scientific bodies in the United States, and had come to similar conclusions as their European counterparts about the substances' toxicity. But it is the Europeans who chose to act. What was perfectly legal in the United States would soon have to be eliminated from electronic devices sold in Europe. All the engineers in that room, like all American high-tech electronics companies, were facing a deadline of July 1, 2006, six months hence.

The high-tech industry is not alone in this quandary. Electronics, automobiles, toys, cosmetics—Europe's new standards are requiring a reassessment of the chemicals inside that make them tick. Evidence has been mounting on both sides of the Atlantic of the troubling effects from exposure to chemicals that are often the secret, unknown ingredient in the products and conveniences of our modern era. Both the United States and Europe are seeing rising rates of infertility among males and females, increasing rates of endocrine-related malformations, and neurological disorders that scientists ascribe to the effects of toxic chemicals. The U.S. Centers for Disease Control tested for 148 toxic chemicals in 2005 and discovered their presence in the bodies of "Americans of all ages."[3] The scientific journal Environmental Health Perspectives, published by the National Institute of Environmental Health Sciences, concluded in 2006 that in developed countries, "Clues from environmental exposure assessments, wildlife studies and animal and human studies hint [that] exposure to low-level contaminants . . . may be subtly undermining our ability to reproduce."[4] Globally, the World Health Organization estimates that the deaths of at least five million people a year can be attributed at least partly to their exposure to toxic chemicals; millions more suffer their debilitating carcinogenic, mutagenic, and neuro-toxic effects. While Europeans have been trying to limit exposure of their citizens to such substances, the Bush administration has led the United States into a retreat from such protections. Now Europe is pre-senting an unprecedented challenge to American industry.

Michael Kirschner, a San Francisco–based engineer and high-tech consultant, had helped organize the gathering to inform his fellow engineers of what they needed to do to meet that looming deadline. "This is an unstoppable force," he said. "This is not some flight of European fancy. It's not going away." Either you get rid of those chemicals, he told them, or give up selling to the Europeans.

For the engineers, not to mention all of Silicon Valley and America's high-tech industry, losing that market would be a disaster. At least one-third of the high-tech industry's $500 billion in annual sales is to Europe. But the news, judging from the nervous uncer-tainty in the room, had yet to sink in.

Kirschner is down-to-earth and friendly. He's stocky and handsome in an almost boyish way, quick to laugh, exuding curiosity and intel-ligence. He worked as an engineer for the Compaq Computer Corp before starting his own firm, Design Chain Associates. It is easy for Kirschner to look at, say, a radio or a DVD player, or something far more complicated like a kidney-dialysis machine, and imagine its insides, the wires and the chips loaded with electrical information that make it work. He's far more accustomed to the dry traffic pat-terns of electrical impulses than the intersections between business and geopolitics. But it was the latter that was catching up with the former—as it was across an array of American businesses. Three years ago Kirschner started seeing the writing on the wall, and decided to make monitoring what the EU would mean for the electronics industry his business. 2006 was a boom year.

The engineers in the Quanta Labs meeting room were accustomed to creative challenges. How to construct and solve mechanical puzzles is something they know well. As Kirschner told me: "These guys have spent their careers thinking creatively about how to solve problems, come up with new ideas, and put them into action." But questioning the potentially toxic chemical properties of all those components they'd been working with was something that their training had never required. It was the end of the era in which what was contained in those products was of no consequence, compared to what they could do. Now someone in Brussels was telling them what to put in the machines they'd spent their careers inventing—or more precisely, what to take out of them.

Kirschner's presentation was a wake-up call. The engineers took careful notes and fired off anxious questions: "What were the chances of getting a waiver?" "How had tin held up as a replacement for lead solder?" "Can we claim hardship and get a six-month delay?" (Answers: Slim. Pretty well. No.)

Kirschner and several other engineer-presenters went through the multiple details of how to ensure compliance with the new standards on the horizon. Then something else he said really jolted them to attention: The next month he would be going to China, where executives in that country's booming high-tech industry had asked him to do a similar briefing.

The Chinese had already written a law based closely on the EU's directive. Who knew how well it would be enforced, but companies had to pay attention: China banned the same substances that had been banned in Europe, so what happened in distant Brussels was taking on global urgency. A whole team of translators was on regular watch in Beijing to translate that and other EU environmental policies into Chinese for review. They had been, one EU diplomat told me, "cherry-picking the best from us." Other major electronics-producing countries, like Korea, Japan, and Taiwan, were following the Europeans too, ratcheting up environmental standards. The one country that did not have such laws was the United States—which has been retreating from such measures while the rest of the world advances. What soon could not be sold in Frankfurt or Tokyo or Beijing could be sold without problem in Houston or Chicago.

The American dream seemed cozy and affluent in that Silicon Valley office park. But power was shifting. You could see it in the faces of those engineers: That anvil could drop any minute.

June 25, 2004, was an election day that most Americans neither noticed nor heard about. On that day, two hundred million Europeans went to the polls in the EU's twenty-five member countries to elect their representatives to the European Parliament.

I watched the returns flickering in that night, on a bank of hastily assembled television screens in the Parliament's elegant, wood-paneled legislative chamber. From Portugal in the west to Latvia in the east, this was the biggest transnational democratic experiment in history. Candidates and their aides from throughout Europe, along with hundreds of reporters and their camera crews from around the world, milled about as tensions rose through the night. There was not, however, an American news anchor to be found, nor more than a handful of American reporters—though the parliamentarians elected that day would become key players in an institution that would soon present major challenges to whomever was elected president five months later in the United States.

Still, while Americans were for the most part oblivious, some were watching closely. Those included officials of the American Electrical Alliance, who knew, like Mike Kirschner, that they would have to prepare their membership for the changes that were coming to their industry. Lobbyists with the American Chemical Council, representing the U.S. chemical industry, were watching, for they were discovering that they had to spend more time worrying about legislation emanating from Brussels than they did from Washington, D.C. Executives with some of America's top cosmetics companies were watching, for they could see that, despite their best efforts, European laws would soon challenge what was in their beauty products. Diplomats from the U.S. mission to the European Union were watching; they had been trying to orchestrate end runs around rising EU authority for the past three years. A posse of public relations experts from Burson-Marsteller, Hill & Knowlton, and other expert opinion shapers and manipulators, representing dozens of U.S. companies, was watching, for the results would determine whom among Europe's 756 legislators they would be courting, and the challenges ahead for their corporate clientele. They, if few others, knew that the consequences of what happened that day would come rippling back across the Atlantic to pose a challenge to fundamental principles of the American economy.

There were others tracking those returns too. The Chinese were watching, for they were beginning to take some of their cues from the Europeans as they try to gradually reshape their roaring economy in a more sustainable direction. And the big regional powers— Brazil, India, South Africa—had their delegates watching carefully in Brussels that day because it was increasingly to Europe that they were looking for new alliances, new trade agreements, and new sources of inspiration for their developing countries.

Strangely enough, all these global players were watching more carefully than most of those whose votes actually counted: Europeans. The turnout across Europe was less than 40 percent, indicating the skepticism with which many Europeans approach the institutions of the EU. Indeed, there was one thing Europeans and Americans shared in common that day: little comprehension of the profound impact their vote would have on the United States.

While Americans slept, a new global force was born. And though they were barely informed of the winners on the following day—the election received just a one-column report on an inside page of the *New York Times*—Americans would nevertheless start feeling the results. The election slightly strengthened the hand of the Christian Democrat–dominated European People's Party, but whoever won was less important than the fact that they were now there.

The parliamentarians elected that day represent the largest and most affluent economy in the world, with a population of 450 million people and a gross domestic product that in 2005 jumped ahead of that of the United States, a gap that has continued to grow as the EU's newest members' economies expand.[5] Two more countries, Romania and Bulgaria, joined the EU in 2007. The EU is now the single largest trading partner with every continent except Australia. That includes countries in America's own backyard: the Mercosur trading bloc of Latin America (Brazil, Argentina, Venezuela, Uruguay, Paraguay, and associate member Chile) conducts more trade with Europe today than it does with their longtime patron, and sometime antagonist, the United States.[6] The ripple effects from this shift in economic power have been some of the big untold changes of the new century. For with wealth comes trade, and from trade comes the power to write the rules of commerce.

Most Americans have missed this hugely transformative process. The United States was once the pioneer of new approaches to environmental protection. In the 1970s and 1980s an American mix of scientific rigor and legal muscle gave birth to a body of environmental regulations and laws that was seen as a model around the world. There were costs, to be sure: compliance with the Clean Air and Clean Water Acts from that period required billions in investments for pollution scrubbers, cleaner gasoline, and new waste-filtration technology. But there was no economic catastrophe, as industry had predicted at the time. New industries were created to develop those and other clean technologies, which cemented U.S. leadership going into the 1990s. Back then, America wrote the rules and the world followed.

But no more; leadership has switched. The European Union is asserting new priorities that are far more protective of citizens' health and the environment than those in the United States and they have the economic muscle to back them up. The strength of the U.S. economy, and the global influence that comes with it, has always been rooted in its enormous three-hundred-million-people-strong home market. Today, Europe presents a market of twenty-seven countries that is significantly larger, both in population and in wealth. Likewise, its export trade has long powered U.S. influence; however, in 2005, according to the CIA's World Factbook, Germany overtook the United States as the world's biggest exporter. The EU has been demanding that its industry take responsibility for the collateral health damages caused by its products, and it has done so with innovations that are leading the world. Americans will be feeling the impact of these changes in power and influence quite personally: in their health and in the health of the environment.

"What's happening today is similar to what happened thirty years ago, only in reverse," commented David Vogel, a professor at the Haas Business School at the University of California–Berkeley who has been studying the interplay between trade and environmental regulations. "In the 1980s, for example, when the United States imposed new fuel-efficiency standards, it took about a day for the Japanese to make those their own. Europeans did the same thing when it came to environmental standards. They made those American standards their own. Well, it's the same thing today, except the Europeans are in the position we were once in. The difference, though, is that we are refusing to adapt, as they once did."[7]

Regardless, the die has been cast. U.S. companies, long accustomed to doing business on their own terms and according to rules they have played a large role in writing, are now faced with a new set of rules reflecting heightened attention to the environmental consequences of their products. "In Europe today we are seeing a focal point of regulatory action other than the United States that, for the first time in the postwar period, is driving world markets," comments David Wirth, a trade-law specialist and director of international programs at Boston College Law School.[8] Wirth served in the State Department in the 1980s, where he helped negotiate the Montreal Protocol, a global treaty aimed at protecting the ozone layer. That effort was led by the United States and established a model for trading pollution credits that is now being adapted by the EU and other signatories to the Kyoto accord to fight global warming—but without U.S. participation. American business has been left struggling to keep up with a multibillion dollar market steeped in the values of sustainable development.

The shrinking of U.S. leadership in environmental regulation is compelling U.S. companies, for the first time in history, to make a decision: either adapt to Europe's more aggressive standards for protecting the health of its citizens, or risk losing what is now the biggest and most affluent market in the world. U.S. companies operating in Europe are frequently responding to that challenge differently abroad than they do at home.

Some of those engineers in Silicon Valley would finally follow Kirschner's advice and take the toxics out of their products. Americans who purchased them would thus find themselves protected by the EU, filling in the vacuum left by the absence of their own government. In this way, Americans are the beneficiaries of market forces emanating from a continent that most will likely never visit, much less learn any of the languages spoken there.

In many other instances, however, the results are far more troubling. Americans are being exposed to hazards from which their European peers are being protected. In one industry after another, a new double standard is emerging: that between the protection offered Europe's citizens, and those afforded to Americans. Repeatedly, American companies that have been forced to meet higher standards in Europe, claim to Americans that they cannot do the same thing back in the United States. Why can't companies do in America what they're already doing in Europe? Why, for just two examples, did toy and cosmetics companies come to the California state capitol in Sacramento and explain to legislators that they cannot produce products as cleanly here as they are already producing them in Europe?

A woman's satchel of cosmetics, for example, may look quite different in Berlin than it does in Boston because the EU has banned hundreds of chemicals from cosmetics and personal-care products that have been determined to be carcinogenic or mutagenic. There is a chance the toys being bounced around by a European infant are less toxic than the toys an infant plays with in the United States, and that the car an infant's parents drive has a far less toxic footprint on the eastern side of the Atlantic than on the western side. European "life-cycle analysis" is revealing how much the profits of U.S. manufacturers of consumer goods are inflated by hiding the real costs of production and "end of life" disposal. Most significantly, a European-led revolution in chemical regulation requires that thousands of chemicals finally be assessed for their potentially toxic effects on human beings, and signals the end of American industry's ability to withhold critical data from the public.

When it comes to chemicals, the Europeans and the Americans disagree fundamentally on what constitutes a risk. The Europeans assess the inherent toxicity of a substance and, based on an accumulation of evidence, determine that its potential to cause harm is enough to remove it from circulation. The Americans have a far higher standard for action, awaiting conclusive scientific evidence of toxic exposure before acting. The frequent result is that the European Union and the United States review the same scientific studies, have access to the same toxicity data, and come to entirely different conclusions. The European approach is called the precautionary principle, and the result is that many substances now banned in Europe are in wide use in the United States.

This conflict over risk—What is it? How much evidence is needed to prove it? How much is enough to prompt the government to act?— is at the core of the different environmental paths followed by the United States and the European Union. Industry generally perceives the Europeans jumping to conclusions before all the evidence is in to satisfy political demands for environmental action. As Becky Linder, International Affairs officer of the American Electrical Association put it to me: "The EU has got to take the science out of politics."[9] Linder was one of those monitoring the election in June 2004; it is her industry that was attending those anxious sessions in Silicon Valley as a result of the European laws she once lobbied against, unsuccessfully, in Brussels. Advocates of the precautionary principle counter that science is always a continuum: one answer leads to another question, which leads to another answer, and so on. As Mike Wilson, an environmental-health scientist at the University of California–Berkeley, who has advocated before Congress that the United States adopt a more precautionary approach, comments: "It's the job of politicians to make a decision somewhere along that continuum."[10] The European Union resolves debates prompted by scientific research in favor of preventing harm before it happens, even if the prospects are uncertain, while the United States seeks an at times elusive certainty. Meanwhile, much of the rest of the world, including the new economic engines like China, increasingly follow Europe's approach, suggesting troubles ahead as their increasingly "green" competitors leave Americans behind.

Efforts to block Europe's precautionary initiatives, and to prevent them from rebounding and gaining a foothold in the United States, are giving American lobbyists reason to travel. As Brussels becomes the new center of the action—and threat—for global business, the number of lobbyists since 2001 has tripled. The largest contingent of non-European lobbyists in Brussels are Americans, many of whom have moved wholesale from Washington to Brussels to try to stop, or slow down, European efforts to "green" the global economy. AmCham EU, an affiliate of the U.S. Chamber of Commerce representing U.S. transnationals operating in Europe, has seen its membership double since 2001. In the process, U.S. companies have had to learn new ways of exerting influence over a governing institution in which the usual cocktail of campaign contributions, arm-twisting, and seduction are often neither warmly received nor, in the case of campaign contributions, legal.

Twenty-five years ago I coauthored, with David Weir, the book *Circle of Poison*,[11] which exposed how American chemical companies were exporting banned pesticides that they were forbidden to sell to Americans. Citizens of developing countries were victims of America's own double standard: they were the market for America's forbidden products because their governments' environmental standards were far weaker than those in the United States. I never imagined that a quarter century later the effect of the U.S. government's withdrawal from serious environmental oversight would be to place Americans at the lower end of another double standard: that between the protections offered to Americans and those offered to their counterparts in Europe and elsewhere in the world. This prompted me to ask: Is America itself becoming a dumping ground for products forbidden because of their toxic effects in other countries?

Coal and steel. Those were the essential ingredients of what is now the European Union, which began with a 1952 pact between France and Germany to permit free trade in the two commodities most critical to postwar reconstruction. Jean Monnet, the postwar French diplomat and visionary behind the "Coal and Steel Pact," saw early on that tying together the fates of Europe's antagonistic powers through economic links was the most effective way to ensure peace, and to navigate the rebuilding of a continent shattered by six years of war. Monnet took the long view; he understood that the European constellation of nation-states, with their conflicting sovereign imperatives, could lead once again to chaos. He envisioned a unified Europe that would both accelerate economic development and wield an influence far greater than the sum of its national parts. The coal and steel deal was the seed from which a new, stronger Europe could emerge. It has taken four decades, and many unexpected turns—the end of the cold war primary among them—but Monnet's vision is coming to fruition.

In 1977, in a fit of pique, Secretary of State Henry Kissinger famously blurted out to an aide: "If I want to pick up the phone and talk to Europe, whom do I call?" Today, the area code for that number is clear: 32-2, for Brussels, and the man at the other end of the line would be José Manuel Barroso, president of the European Commission, the EU's executive branch. Behind him rests the twenty-seven-member Council of Ministers, with a single representative from each member state (who elected Barroso), and the European Parliament, with members (MEPs) elected directly within the member states. Behind that three-branch governing structure, bearing not unintentional resemblance to that of the United States, rests not armies, but the accumulated power of 480 million of the wealthiest and best-educated consumers and producers in the world.[12]

Several years after Kissinger's exclamation, starting in the mid-1980s, I was based in Paris and began traveling to Brussels on reporting forays. I'd drop in to interview members of the European Parliament, who in those days had little political clout. Europe's early crop of elected representatives, however, did have access to information, and a generous willingness to offer an inside look at

European-American disputes of the time. I have been returning to Brussels periodically ever since, and have visited the successors of those MEPs, who have evolved from being back-channel sources of sensitive information about the United States to being active participants in the shaping of legislation that, in many instances, is actually changing the United States.

After the end of the cold war, European diplomats gathered in the Dutch city of Maastricht to sign a treaty, dubbed the "Single European Act." Known in the Eurocrat vernacular as simply "Maastricht," the treaty propelled the EU from being primarily a free-trade zone—then called the European Community—into a unified government force with the legal teeth to back up its actions. Bo Manderup Jensen, principal adviser on parliamentary affairs to the European Commission, explained to me that it was then that the EU we see today began to take form. Maastricht dramatically expanded the EU's authority. Over the following fifteen years, the EU member states, Jensen said, ceded three quarters of their governing mandate to Brussels, in areas ranging from environmental regulation to food safety, accounting standards, telecommunications policy, and oversight of corporate mergers.[13]

Until then, advanced environmental thinking was pretty much limited to the national level in countries like Germany, the Netherlands, and Scandinavia. But after Maastricht, those ideas started filtering their way into the EU. The influence of the Greens and Europe's growing environmental movement were felt across the continent. Though the Greens' legislative presence has rarely exceeded 10 percent on either a national or EU level, they have frequently leveraged their numbers into alliances with European Socialist parties to push an environmental agenda. By 2002, the European Commission had issued a report calling for "sustainable and environmentally sound" principles—including "life-cycle analysis"—to be integrated into all EU policies alongside "competitiveness" of European industry. These underlying principles would later bear fruit in the initiatives we are seeing today.

The election of June 2004 was the first to include the EU's ten newest members, most of them formerly communist countries to the east. All of the EU's member countries have opted to merge their national identities into a single web of economic and political inter-connections, the foundation for a historic democratic experiment in transnational government. Its architects have been well aware of the EU's departure from the usual march of political history: Jacques Delors, the visionary European Commission president from 1985 to 1994, used to refer lightheartedly to the evolving union as an "Unidentified Political Object."

Political scientists call Europe's form of influence "soft power," exerted not through military might but through the lure of its vast market and from less tangible qualities of moral leadership. But there's a hard edge to the EU's soft power. That edge was discovered with a jolt by Microsoft, which was fined close to a billion dollars for violating European principles of fair competition in its mar-keting of computer software; by General Electric, which had its pro-posed merger with Honeywell blocked because of similar anticompetitiveness concerns; and by Philip Morris, which agreed to a one billion dollar fine to settle allegations of tobacco smuggling and evading taxes. These were warning shots, showing that changing European standards of competition and corporate fraud were no longer a matter of quaint differences of perspective, but had the teeth of enforcement behind them. Now some of those teeth are being put behind environmental protection.

It would be hard to invent a more fitting choice of street names to convey the changing role between Brussels and Washington, than those of the two streets that converge in the former working-class neighborhood in the southeast of the city, now transformed into the seat of EU power. The rue Monnet, as in Jean, and the rue Franklin, as in Benjamin, meet under the shadows of the four-pronged star of concrete and steel that is home to the Berlaymont, headquarters of the European Commission. The parallels between those two luminaries of European and American history, two hundred years apart, seem to many in Brussels abundantly clear.

I took a stroll through the neighborhood with Frank Schwalba-Hoth, the European Parliament's first Green MEP, who now works as a consultant for foreign governments in their interactions with the EU. We passed venerable old working-class pubs, now competing with high-end restaurants and gourmet cheese shops appealing to the Eurocrats who pour onto these streets every day. "The last fifty years in Europe have been like the year 1775 in the United States," he said. "Who in the world was aware of what was happening in the U.S. in the years before 1776? Then in 1776, everyone knew. What is happening now in Europe is our 1776."[14]

The man charged with explaining the implications of Europe's innovations to Americans is Robert Donkers. Trained as an environmental economist in his native Netherlands, Donkers went to Brussels in 1982 to work with the practically brand new Environment Directorate, which had barely a hundred employees. In those days, what was then known as the European Community had just nine members and little power; it was primarily a free-trade zone for its member-countries.

Donkers' gregarious personality and thick gray beard suggest a ship captain in a suit. Over nearly two decades, he served in the Environment Directorate as it went from being a largely symbolic presence—responsible mainly for delivering studies on things like transport policy—to being responsible for writing and monitoring the enforcement of some of the most comprehensive environmental legislation in the world today. In 2004, Donkers was posted to Washington as the EU's environment counselor to the United States.

His position is a first in international diplomacy, reflecting the profound changes in consciousness around the role played by environmental considerations in mapping our economic future.

"They asked me to please explain to whomever wants to listen in America, what we're doing in Europe on chemicals and climate change," Donkers told me. "And, second, to inform us [in Brussels] what is happening in the United States. We know that there is a different America out there than the views expressed by President Bush on the environment."[15]

Donkers has traveled the country, talking with representatives of every conceivable industry—chemical, electronic, plastic, cosmetic, aerospace, automobile, medical, and countless others—who are the primary producers and consumers of chemicals that are being placed under more stringent review in Europe. He has met repeatedly with members of Congress and their staffs, and with officials in the government—in the Environmental Protection Agency, in the State and Commerce departments, and with the U.S. trade representative—as well as with nongovernmental organizations (NGOs) inspired by the model being set by the EU. In the process, Donkers has discovered that the United States is indeed not only the Bush administration, but also a country hungry for new means of breaking the stalemate that has long characterized efforts at environmental reform. This includes business people who see flaws in the shortsighted perspective now dominating Washington, and with state officials who, in the absence of federal leadership, are taking matters into their own hands and looking beyond Washington toward Brussels as a source of inspiration for environmental initiatives in state capitals across the country. Donkers told me that he had become an "environmental Mohican"—a rare diplomat whose portfolio is promoting Europe's ideas of environmental protection.

Transatlantic trade accounts for about 40 percent of all global commerce: the United States and Europe, still each other's most significant trading partners, are caught up in a mutually reinforcing loop of common history, economic interchange, and competition. This book includes dispatches from the friction points in that evolving relationship. It has a foot on either side of the Atlantic, investigating the reverberations from Brussels to Washington and beyond. "When Washington sneezes," the saying used to go, "Europe catches a cold." Today, that clever aphorism seems as out of date as the cold that was once a war.

The hands on the levers of power are shifting. The business community has been aware of this changing dynamic long in advance of the public. An entirely new position, the standards liaison, was created inside the Department of Commerce in 2003 to monitor the new environmental and other standards that are proliferating in Europe and elsewhere around the world, and presenting potential threats to American exports.[16]

Penelope Naas watched these changes unfold, as director for EU and Regional Affairs at the Commerce Department from 2003 to 2006, when she left government to take a job as a senior vice president for international affairs at Citibank. Naas used to go to Brussels at least "once a month," she told me, to express America's rising resistance to Brussels' more assertive approach to environmental regulation. She frequently sat across the table from Robert Donkers in Washington, to express the government's concerns. From her office at Citibank, she recalled those days of helping to lead U.S. opposition. "The biggest change I saw was what it means for the U.S. to be overtaken as the world's largest economy." She told me it was clear that Europe would be willing to challenge U.S. leadership on everything from "new financial accounting standards" to the "safety of boilers" to "requirements for the toxic screening of chemicals." Naas' concern was that this shift in power could have long-term effects on America's global competitive edge. "Down the road," she said, "things are going to get tough for us."[17]

2

The Beauty Bluff

The Fabrics and Home Care division for Procter & Gamble in northern Europe is an island of calm on the northwest edge of Brussels. In 1958, this leafy five-acre parcel was home to the Belgian-hosted World's Fair, but since 1966 it has been an innovation and product-development center for the world's largest consumer-products company. A glass case in the foyer features a collection of Procter & Gamble's array of familiar products: a Head & Shoulders shampoo bottle, Mr. Clean household cleanser (M. Propre in its French variation), Gillette razor blades and shaving cream, a canister of Pringles, a box of Ariel detergent. The week before I visited, Procter & Gamble had bought another giant of the industry, Gillette. It is safe to say that Procter & Gamble has a presence in almost every American and European home. It's the quintessential transnational consumer-products company—and thus must contend with the at times competing demands of different government authorities, the two most significant of which are the European Union and the United States.

I was greeted by Joris Pollet, a genial Belgian who is the company's associate director for corporate external relations in Europe, Africa, and the Middle East, and his British colleague in the external-relations department, Lucy Hodgson. They walked me along shaded pathways reminiscent of a community-college campus—past low-slung buildings now filled with scientists, pollsters, and sales representatives, the men and women behind one of the biggest chemical users for consumer products on earth. Inside those buildings, the company conducts confidential experiments to come up with the next wave of new or improved products. With some seven thousand scouts involved in a continuous stream of market surveys and national-trend studies in more than a hundred countries, Procter & Gamble, like any multinational firm, has always contended with a multiplicity of tax and tariff structures, measurement standards, distribution systems, labeling requirements, and, not least of all, national tastes.

"We are global, but we think local," Pollet commented.[1] As an example of what he called the company's "glocalism," he cited market surveys in Italy which suggested that a newly developed pizza-flavored Pringle would not receive a positive response among Italians: "We discovered that it would never work in Italy. Among Italians, pizza is part of the national heritage. Their mother and their grandmothers make it at home. They did not want to taste it on our Pringles." Alas, the pizza-flavored Pringle rollout never happened in Italy, but in the United Kingdom and the United States, the snacks have been a hit. "Mmmm, they're delicious," puckered Lucy Hodgson. Among other such discoveries of local habits to which the company has adapted: the Poles tend to use far less laundry detergent per load than their far more affluent neighbors, the Germans, who tend to overdose their clothes. Thus, a slightly more concentrated Ariel was developed for Poland, a slightly weaker version for the Germans. The same principle of "glocalism," I would discover, applies to the divergent health standards of the two largest blocs of consumers of Procter & Gamble's product lines: Europeans and Americans.

The three of us sat down to lunch in the company cafeteria, in a tranquil setting alongside a small pond loaded with colorful tropical fish. It was "Fair Trade" week in Belgium. Procter & Gamble, like other companies, was participating in a countrywide effort to highlight how trade could be used to raise the living standards of people in developing countries. As we munched on a tasty Caribbean chicken dish featuring "Oxfam raisins"—a fair-trade import by the British charity, Oxfam—Pollet explained that differing standards have long been at the forefront of concerns for a company with the marketing breadth of Procter & Gamble. Most of those, he said, have to do with "measurements, packaging, that kind of thing." For a company with 687 different products, marketed in 140 different countries, that can present a logistical challenge, and one that it has clearly mastered: Procter & Gamble, founded in 1837, is one of the most consistently profitable companies in the personal-care industry.

But Procter & Gamble, and other companies like it, are now facing a far greater challenge to their global marketing strategies than any of those logistical puzzles. Over the past decade, concern has mounted over the potentially toxic effects of chemicals contained in all those crèmes and lotions, brushed-on colors, adhesive nail polishes, and creamy shampoos. The average American adult is exposed to more than one hundred distinct chemicals from personal-care products every day.[2]

Chronic chemical exposure generally occurs in minute quantities that accrue over time; assessing their precise effect is extremely difficult. But the sheer abundance of toxins to which women are routinely exposed—through cosmetics as well as numerous other products—prompted the Breast Cancer Fund, a nonprofit group of health-care advocates, to assert that as many as one-half of new breast cancer cases cannot be explained by known risk factors, such as genetic predisposition, smoking, or estrogen hormone-replacement therapies. The group claims that chemicals may be a significant contributing factor.[3] A study by the University of Southern California School of Medicine concluded that women who use hair dyes at least once a month for a year are twice as likely to develop bladder cancer than women who do not; those who use it for fifteen years or longer face triple the risk.[4] The Center for Environmental Oncology at the University of Pittsburgh Cancer Institute cautions that some substances in cosmetics mimic the female hormone estrogen, and that such additives in hair-care products may be contributing to otherwise inexplicable incidences of breast cancer among African American women (the primary users of such hair treatments) under the age of forty.[5] Other common substances in cosmetics include what a growing number of scientists suggest may be endocrine-disrupting chemicals, mutagens, and reproductive toxins.

So in March 2005, when the seventh amendment to the EU's Cosmetics Directive (originally passed in 1976)) came into force, requiring that all "products intended to be placed in contact with the various external parts of the human body" would henceforth be subject to scientific review, a message came out of every bottle and tube. The mystery behind beauty products' magic was laid bare: Cosmetics are far more dependent on synthetic chemicals than on natural "essences" of anything. The seventh amendment mandates that chemicals determined to be carcinogens, mutagens, or reproductive toxins—known collectively as CMRs—be removed from cosmetics sold in Europe[6] (It also mandates a phase-out in the testing of cosmetic ingredients on animals.)

Amendment seems almost too soft a word to evoke the radical impact the Europeans are having on the multibillion-dollar global cosmetics industry. These were standards of an entirely different order than those to which Procter & Gamble and every other cosmetics producer had long been accustomed. Until then, the health implications of the 10,500 ingredients that the Food and Drug Admiinistration says are contained in cosmetic and personal-care products were given little attention on either side of the Atlantic. Procter & Gamble, like hundreds of other cosmetic companies operating in Europe, was for the first time compelled to prepare "safety portfolios," to be made available on demand to European health authorities, for the ingredients in its mascara, lipstick, hair dye, shampoo, shaving cream, skin cream, perfume, deodorants, nail polish, tanning lotion, and other products. Every quarter, a committee of toxicologists drawn from universities and laboratories across Europe, known as the Scientific Committee on Cosmetic Products, convenes in Brussels to review those ingredients. Those put on what's known as a "negative list"—including the CMRs—cannot be sold in Europe. Another "restricted" list includes ingredients for which uses are severely limited.[7]

By the end of 2006, the negative list had grown from four hundred to more than eleven hundred substances. Many of the chemicals on the negative list, like arsenic and even various forms of jet fuel, for example, are never used in cosmetics. Nor does the EU, like the U.S., require premarket approval of cosmetic ingredients. What it does do, however, is clarify what ingredients are not permitted in cosmetics—namely, those that may contribute to cancer, may have mutagenic effects, or may damage the reproductive system. Procter & Gamble hired a staff of compliance officers and lawyers responsible for ensuring its ingredients passed the Europeans' new toxicity screen. "We comply with the laws wherever we operate," Pollet said. Indeed, his company has rarely been brought to court for violating either EU or U.S. laws pertaining to the safety of its products. Procter & Gamble submitted "mountains" of toxicity data, according to Pollet, about the vast array of chemicals it uses—and has found appropriate alternatives for those it has been forced to remove.

"And what," I asked, "about the United States?" The United States remains Procter & Gamble's largest market. All of the company's products are approved for their journey into the marketplace from

Procter & Gamble's global headquarters in Cincinnati, Ohio. Pollet, not an expert in U.S. law, paused; he cut into his Oxfam-raisin-seasoned chicken. "That's a difficult question," he said.

Every morning across America, tens of millions of women apply from twelve to twenty "personal-care" products to themselves, according to the Cosmetic, Toiletry and Fragrance Association (CTFA). From tubes and bottles and delicate brushes come the tools of beauty, hygiene, and self-preservation known as cosmetics. American women might assume that somebody has been watching to ensure that potential toxins in those ingredients are kept away from intimate contact with the body's largest organ, the skin. They would be wrong. The FDA provides oversight and monitoring of over-the-counter and prescription drugs, as well as food additives, but it has minimal authority to regulate the ingredients in cosmetics.

"Women believe that the government which they think is there is actually there," comments Charlotte Brody, a registered nurse and executive director of Commonweal, an environmental-health organization. "But it's not there."[8]

Back in 1938, when the mandate of the Food and Drug Administration was expanded by Congress to give it authority over drugs and food additives, industry lobbying succeeded in blocking the agency from requiring testing of cosmetics. That hasn't changed for seventy years. Procter & Gamble and other industry giants—like Revlon, Unilever, Estée Lauder, and others—have successfully opposed every effort to broaden the FDA's mandate to include cosmetics. Since the governing principles of the FDA were established some seventy years ago, entirely new disciplines of science have emerged to study the long-term effects of chemicals on the human body. But the FDA's authority over these substances has changed little. This vacuum at the heart of America's regulatory apparatus is not difficult to discover: it's right on the agency's Web Site. "FDA's legal authority over cosmetics is different from other products regulated by the agency, such as drugs, biologics, and medical devices," reads a statement by the agency's Bureau of Colors and Cosmetics. "Cosmetic products and ingredients are not subject to FDA pre-market approval authority. . . . Cosmetic firms are responsible for substantiating the safety of their products and ingredients before marketing."[9] The FDA makes one exception to this open door: it does require premarketing review for color additives.

The closest U.S. equivalent to the EU's "scientific committees" comes not from government, but from the industry's lobbying and public-relations arm. In 1976, as Congress debated strengthening the mandate of the FDA, the CTFA argued to maintain its exemption from scrutiny and promised to police itself. The trade group created a Cosmetics Ingredient Review (CIR) board, a panel of scientists that convenes three times a year in Washington to review the literature on chemicals used in cosmetics. The panel is financed entirely by the CTFA's member companies. Their recommendations to the industry are only that—and are not necessarily listened to in any case. The CIR's opinions are available on the Web; they list several ingredients that the board identified as substances of concern that have yet to be removed from U.S. cosmetics.[10] These include coal tar, a black hair dye that the University of Southern California School of Medicine says may be linked to bladder cancer among hairdressers and is still used in many low-cost beauty salons; and sodium borate, sometimes called boric acid, which has been linked to testicular development problems and which the CIR recommended "should not be used on infant or injured skin," and is an ingredient in Desitin diaper-rash lotion for infants, according to a Household Products Database maintained by the U.S. National Library of Medicine.[11]

By contrast, in Europe the scientific committees deliver their findings to the Health and Consumer Protection Directorate, the EU body charged with overseeing consumer-product safety, which determines what if any action to take if a risk has been identified. The critical distinction between the U.S. and European systems, according to David Vogel, the University of California–Berkeley economist who has compared the approaches to cosmetic regulation, is that in Europe scientists act independently of the government or industry, and politicians, operating under the precautionary principle, may take action on potential risks even before an absolute scientific consensus has been reached.[12]

In the United States, however, there is no disinterested party assessing a product's potential toxicity before it is sold and ultimately applied to your skin. That doesn't mean that a product is unsafe, but neither is there any independent affirmation that it is safe. One FDA rule, for example, requires that warning labels be put on products that contain ingredients "whose safety has not been determined." But it is the cosmetic companies, not the FDA, that make that determination. While the cosmetic companies assert that their products are safe, 89 percent of the ingredients used in cosmetics today have not been assessed by either the FDA or by industry.[13] Nor are there clear guidelines defining what is meant by "safe." When it comes to chemicals in food, for example, the Environmental Protection Agency is mandated to impose restrictions on pesticides to ensure that the danger of getting cancer from exposure to a carcinogenic pesticide is limited to one in one million. No such standards are applied to cosmetics. Jane Houlihan, an environmental engineer and research director at the Environmental Working Group, a Washington, D.C.–based NGO, characterizes the ingredient-review board's focus as emphasizing acute symptoms, rather than more chronic, accumulative health effects. "The [CIR] boards look at things like eye and skin irritation, factors which most directly affect what people buy, and not what the long-term implications might be."[14]

John Bailey, a chemist and former director of the FDA's Office of Cosmetics and Colors, who is now executive vice president for science at the CTFA, disputes that description. In a telephone interview in April 2007, he told me that the CIR's seven members—three dermatologists, two toxicologists, a nutritional scientist, and a veterinarian— "are knowledgeable about risk and risk assessments. If you have a checklist, you don't need experts. Experts apply their expert knowledge, and their findings are disseminated to the world."[15]

The seventh amendment to the EU's Cometics Directive spoiled the laissez-faire party that the cosmetic industry had enjoyed around the world for the better part of a century. Those ingredient reviews never conducted by the FDA in Washington are now being conducted by the "scientific committees," overseen by the Health and Consumer Protection Directorate in Brussels. Their results are posted publicly on the Web.[16] You can take a look yourself and check the ingredient lists on the tubes and bottles on your own bathroom shelf against the toxicity reviews conducted by the European Union.

When the Environmental Working Group (EWG) compared the ingredient lists in over fourteen thousand personal-care products to lists of potential chemical hazards compiled by the EPA, FDA, the International Agency for Research on Cancer, the European Chemicals Bureau, and thirty other scientific and regulatory institutions around the world, their discoveries were a revelation. The EWG found hundreds of varieties of skin and tanning lotions, nail polish and mascara and other personal-care products that contain known or possible carcinogens, mutagens, and reproductive toxins. Ninety-nine percent of the products on the market contained one or more ingredients that had "never been publicly assessed for safety." Sixty percent of the products tested contained potential endocrine disrupters, and a third had ingredients that "limited evidence" suggested could be carcinogens. No one before had even looked.[17]

The EU's demands for toxicity data has complicated life for Procter & Gamble and other cosmetic companies that have long been insulated from government oversight. "The seventh amendment has made more work for our product-development people," Tim Long, Procter & Gamble's manager for Technical External Relations in Cincinnati told me in a December 2006 phone interview from company headquarters in Cincinnati. "It's the cost of doing business. . . . We've got to find substitutes, or just take those things out." "Those things" are the chemicals on the EU's negative list.[18]

Long told me that this did not necessarily mean that the substances the company was removing in Europe were also being removed from similar products in the United States. He said at the time that there may be "slight differences" in the chemical composition of cosmetics sold by the company to Europeans and those sold to Americans, but that the numbers of such parallel product lines were "minuscule compared to our overall product development." He cited one example: that of dibutyl phthalate (DBP), a plastic additive in the company's Cover Girl nail polish that the European Commission put on the negative list as a potential carcinogen. In 2006, the company removed the substance from its nail polishes in Europe but not in the United States. Just as it reconfigured the strength of detergent to satisfy different consumer desires, cosmetic products were being formulated differently to meet the needs, said Long, "of different national regulations."

Long stressed, however, that the company nevertheless disputes the European's assessment of chemical risks—from that substance or any other ingredients singled out by the Europeans. "Even though we disagree with the Europeans' approach," he said, "we abide by it [in Europe]. But appearing on the negative list is not the death knell for a product. We're not concerned if something is on the [Europeans'] list because we believe the ingredients in our products are safe." He said that Procter & Gamble has "hundreds of toxicologists and safety experts" whose job it is to verify the safety of the company's products.

How could the two most advanced and affluent economic systems in the world, with similar consumption patterns and tastes, differ so profoundly on what, exactly, is considered "safe"? This is not an abstract question for the hundreds of millions of people who use cosmetic and personal care products every day. In the United States, the very absence of the FDA in regulating cosmetics suggests (to the public anyway) its implicit endorsement of their safety. The United States relies on industry to determine otherwise. In Europe, the government has thrown those very same ingredients up for independent review and mandated that industry adjust its formulations accordingly.

Long had spent fifteen years as a toxicologist at Procter & Gamble before shifting into his current position. I asked him how such varying interpretations of the same question of safety could now confront his most transnational of companies. "Appearing on someone's list," he said, "does not mean a chemical is dangerous in the circumstances in which it is used." The Europeans, in other words, look at the inherent toxic properties of a substance; the Americans look at how one might actually be exposed. Long explained the difference with a parable: "Imagine," he said, "you encounter a tiger in the wild, and then encounter another tiger behind its protective enclosure in a zoo." The wild tiger, he said, "is inherently dangerous." Get close enough, and it can kill you." Put that tiger behind bars in a zoo, however, and that tiger "is not dangerous at all." Chemicals, Long said, are the tigers in this equation. "It's the same thing in [cosmetic] products," he said. "There may be inherent toxicity to a particular chemical, but if you use it under certain conditions the exposure is minimal and they present no risk." This distinction lies at the core of the disagreement between the two continents in determining chemical safety.

What the Europeans say on this matter is increasingly important. Forty to sixty percent of Procter & Gamble's $56 billion in yearly sales is to overseas markets, according to Long, the largest of which is Europe. The major cosmetic companies—Revlon, Estée Lauder, and other brand-name enterprises—also rely on the European and other overseas markets for a significant portion of their yearly sales. For the cosmetics industry overall, much of their product line is not subject to U.S. regulations at all. Francine Lamoriello, a vice president for global strategies at CTFA, told me that a good number of the association's membership comes from Europe and elsewhere, including L'Oréal from France, Unilever from the Netherlands, and Shiseido from Japan; Brazilian, Korean, Dominican, Peruvian, and other international companies are also among its membership. "Companies have to decide," she said, "whether to formulate everywhere for the European market, or segregate the European market and formulate around it."[19] The seventh amendment prompted every major multinational cosmetic company to face this decision.

Much of the world is now departing from the American laissez-faire approach to potential cosmetic hazards. The United States is finding itself isolated as public anxiety rises over the potential long-term health effects of chemically based cosmetics, and the European way of assessing safety spreads globally. Canada has an "ingredient hotlist" of banned and restricted substances that closely parallels that of the EU. Japan has similar legislation on the books, which in some instances is actually more restrictive than that of the European Union. Argentina and Brazil have been devising new laws based largely on the principles of the Cosmetics Directive. This year China instituted a list of forbidden chemicals in cosmetics based almost entirely on the EU's negative list. After newspapers in Korea publicized the EWG's report, thousands of irate women converged outside the corporate offices of Unilever in Seoul, the nation's capital. The demonstrations prompted the head of the Korean Food and Drug Administration to fly to Washington to express his concerns to his American counterpart. He also met with Charlotte Brody, the nurse who works with the health NGO Commonweal, and other activists. The Koreans shortly thereafter imposed more stringent oversight over cosmetic ingredients than the U.S. Food and Drug Administration, which had originally given the agency, in the aftermath of the Korean War, its name and mandate. The Koreans based their reforms largely on the guidelines contained in the seventh amendment.

Four months after my initial conversation with Dr. Long, I called him again. The company had noticed the changing international climate around cosmetic regulation. "More and more countries outside the United States," he told me, "are leaning toward adopting the EU's procedures. China is even leaning toward the European approach to cosmetics. . . . And that's a pretty big country; they have one in five consumers in the world." In 2007, he said, Procter & Gamble changed its policy to reflect this global shift. The company began formulating according to a single standard, that established by the European Union. "We will no longer use anything on the EU's banned list," he said. The EU would henceforth "provide the basic guidance for our product formulation," as would all recommendations from the Cosmetic Ingredient Review boards, which it agreed to abide by in every instance. The company issued a statement to that effect on the Web site of its British subsidiary. That dibutyl phthalate in its Cover Girl nail polish, he said, was now being taken out of its U.S. Cover Girl formulation, though he insisted the company still does not believe the substance was dangerous. He said the switch was because "American consumers expressed a preference for the European version over our American formulation."[20]

"Glocalism" was taking a curious turn: The EU's Health and Consumer Protection Directorate was, in effect, displacing the FDA as the reigning authority governing cosmetic formulation. But that does not mean that Procter & Gamble, or the industry in general, agrees with the principles being established in Brussels. As I was sitting with Joris Pollet at Procter & Gamble's northern European headquarters in the fall of 2005 and heard of the company's avid compliance with the new EU rules, an entirely different story was unfolding seven thousand miles away. In California, the CTFA was channeling $600,000 into an aggressive lobbying campaign to kill an effort by legislators to require that carcinogenic or reproductively toxic chemicals in cosmetics be disclosed to state health authorities. The proposal, called the Safe Cosmetics Act, was inspired by the Cosmetics Directive. Health advocates wanted to know which, if any, of the substances the state had already listed as carcinogens, mutagens, and reproductive toxins—which it had been required to do by state voters in 1986—were contained in cosmetics. The bill was really a mere shadow of its far more stringent European progenitor. The Europeans list the carcinogens and mutagens that are prohibited from use in cosmetics; the bill's advocates wanted only that the industry provide notification to the state of their presence.

Nevertheless, every major U.S. cosmetic company appeared in Sacramento to oppose the bill—including Revlon, L'Oréal, Estée Lauder and Procter & Gamble, which was the single biggest industry contributor to the CTFA's effort. The company spent more than $200,000 lobbying the state legislature that year,[21] and was a major contributor to a CTFA campaign that included newspaper ads, a Web site,[22] and intensive lobbying of the legislators. Procter & Gamble's Tim Long took the lead in expressing the industry's opposition. "There is no evidence that ingredients in cosmetics are linked to cancer, let alone breast cancer," he testified to the senate health committee. "Our products are very safe."[23]

As Long spoke, some of the ingredients he referred to, those which would have to be reported to the state health authorities, were already in the process of being taken off the market in Europe by his own company, as well as by other U.S. exporters lobbying against the measure. Substitutions were being found. Data was already prepared for the EU's Health and Consumer Affairs Directorate; it must be supplied on demand to national health authorities. In Europe, Procter & Gamble, like other big American companies, was collecting toxicity data that in California the industry claimed would be an "unreasonable and unnecessary regulatory burden" to supply. Few Americans were aware of this seeming contradiction. But then, what American keeps track of chemical regulations when they're on a trip to Europe?

Janet Nudelman, program director of the Breast Cancer Fund, is one of the few. The fund was founded in 1992 to foster public awareness and support for research into the causes of the rising incidences of breast cancer, as well as nontoxic treatments for the disease. Nudelman helped design the fund's Safe Cosmetics Campaign, which has run head-on into the evolving double standard between Europe and the United States. "The industry has been trying to prevent a domino effect from California," she told me, "trying to stop the states from taking regulatory authority where the FDA refuses to go." The first domino in that slow-moving cascade, she said, came from Europe. "They [the cosmetic companies] are spending hundreds of thousands of dollars to lobby against laws in the United States that they've already agreed to in Europe."[24]

The Campaign for Safe Cosmetics asked all companies selling cosmetics in the United States to sign a pact agreeing to abide voluntarily by guidelines based on the EU's restrictions, and to remove toxic ingredients from their products by 2008. The request has divided the industry. Four hundred companies, most of them small to medium-sized natural-cosmetic firms that had already committed to removing potential toxins from their products, agreed to sign, including Avalon Natural Products, Pangea Organics, and The Body Shop. After intense public pressure, Revlon and L'Oréal declined to sign the pact but informed the campaign that formulations for its products sold in the United States would follow European Union guidelines. Procter & Gamble did not sign, though it now cites the

EU as, in effect, the primary government regulatory body for the products it sells to Americans and others around the world.

The Safe Cosmetics Act was ultimately passed by the state legislature, despite the industry's strenuous opposition. Governor Arnold Schwarzenegger's initial resistance was overcome by a coalition of nurses, doctors, environmental-health advocates, and the appearance of none other than Miss Teen World, who showed up at the doorstep of Schwarzenegger's office in Sacramento and pleaded with one of his aides for the governor to sign the act. By early 2007, representatives from CTFA were traveling to Sacramento to work out the details on reporting with the state Health Department. But opposition to the principles of transparency has not softened: "We'd prefer not to have fifty FDAs with different rules," commented John Bailey of the CTFA during our phone interview in April 2007. "That makes business a lot more complicated than it has to be for bringing products safely and promptly to consumers." Would the industry, I asked, prefer to see such standards on a national level? "No," he replied. "There is no compelling health reason to do that. Cosmetics are safe. There have been no major problems with the existing law since it was implemented in 1938."

Reformulating products according to the guidelines of the Cosmetics Directive does not appear to have had a measurable effect thus far on the bottom line. Procter & Gamble showed one of its most profitable years ever in the year following implementation of the seventh amendment; its profits rose 21 percent in 2006.[25]

The one significant player notably absent from this still-ongoing reform of the global cosmetics industry is the FDA, which continues to operate with limited policing powers while many of America's economic peers and competitors increase oversight. In the process, the FDA is becoming less relevant to the production decisions of a major business that literally touches almost every American daily.

After lunch, Joris Pollet and I strolled along those pleasant pathways on Procter & Gamble's Brussels "campus." We passed laboratories where, Pollet admonished me, the product experiments within were "confidential." Inside, somewhere in those buildings, scientists were compiling the data being demanded by the European authorities. I asked Pollet why the company was lobbying against laws to protect consumers in the United States that it's clearly already conceded (by the very act of staying profitably in business) are workable in Europe?

His answer surprised me. Pollet said that such laws were not needed because of critical differences between the legal systems in Europe and the United States. "The United States is a litigious society," he said. "That acts as a reality check."

This response would surprise me less and less as I began to hear a similar refrain from other American companies operating in Europe. When I asked Timothy Long in Cincinnati the same question some months later, Long's answer echoed that of his Belgian colleague. Procter & Gamble opposed the Safe Cosmetics Act, he said, because, "there is a lot of concern that if information like that gets out to the public, there will be bounty hunters looking to sue the companies, and drag us out in litigation."

The United States has long had two legs to its structure of consumer protections: regulation on the one hand, and a receptive legal system on the other, giving citizens the right to pursue redress in the courts as a means of obtaining both compensation and punishment for damages to their or their community's health and environment. The EU has few similar legal mechanisms; citizen standing on liability cases is limited, and damage awards are generally small. In Europe, government is generally presumed to be the first and last line of defense. Principles of European regulation are generally aimed at preventing abuses before they occur. In the United States, regulations may not be as rigorous, goes an argument that I heard many times, but the willingness of the U.S. courts to impose financial sanctions against corporations that cause health or environmental damage provide a sort of after-the-fact penalty. This, as Pollet and Long suggest, acts as a disincentive to abusive practices. Indeed, when the *Sacramento Bee* interviewed Randy Pollock, a lobbyist for the CTFA—whose biggest member is Procter & Gamble—he commented that the Safe Cosmetics Act was unnecessary because of the abundance of "trial attorneys." It was attorneys pursuing legal redress according to the laws of liability in the United States, he told the newspaper, which ensures that, "If there's really a danger of cosmetics, you're going to know fairly quickly."[26]

Such principles of legal liability, known as "torts," are indeed a distinctly American innovation. For two hundred years, the principle of not just compensatory but punitive damages has been an important check on companies that produce goods that cause damage to their users. The legal trail dates as far back as 1791, when a New Jersey court ruled that the task of the jury is, "to give damages for example's sake, to prevent such offences in [the] future. . . . Such a sum . . . would mark [the jury's] disapprobation, and be an example to others."[27]

In more recent times, the litany of corporations found liable for significant financial punishment has been long, including Dow Corning (silicone breast implants), Merck (Vioxx pain reliever), the Ford Motor Company (the "exploding" Pinto), AH Robins (the Dalkon Shield contraceptive), WR Grace (asbestos), and Philip Morris (tobacco). These and many other companies have paid the price—both literally in verdicts costing hundreds of millions or billions of dollars, and in the court of public opinion—for damages wrought by their products. The specter of committed lawyers, representing victims or their survivors, has over the years no doubt impelled producers to assess the costs of producing potentially harmful products and likely, in some instances, discouraged them from doing so. An American, not to mention a Belgian, might even be forgiven for taking comfort in our "litigious society" as a backstop against the weakening of the country's regulatory forces by the Bush administration.

But transatlantic ignorance can cut both ways. Pollet, anyway, could not be expected to know that back in the United States his employer has been one of the leading backers of a nationwide campaign to weaken that critical second limb of consumer protection. Over the past decade, Procter & Gamble has been a major contributor to efforts by American corporations to limit the ability of citizens to sue companies for harm done by their products, and to limit damage awards when and if they lose.

Much of that effort has been focused on judicial races in the states, where product-liability cases are most frequently heard. The company has been a major contributor to a $100 million campaign by the Chamber of Commerce to elect state judges and state attorneys general who are sympathetic to its desire for "tort reform." During the 2004 election year, Procter & Gamble donated $160,000 to a Chamber campaign for four judges running for state supreme court judgeships in its home state of Ohio, who were promoted by the Republican Party as supporters of "tort reform."[28] The American Bar Association later issued a statement criticizing the Chamber for "waging war on the judges who protect the rights and safety of Americans." Procter & Gamble's commitment to dismantling the system cited by both Pollet and Long goes back at least to 1998, when the Public Interest Research Group identified the company as one of the top ten corporate donors to a campaign pressuring Congress to pass a bill that intended to limit damage awards and make it harder for victims to sue.[29] The company contributed $1.6 million to a lobbying campaign by the Chamber of Commerce in favor of the bill, which was ultimately vetoed by President Clinton. Procter & Gamble was also a major supporter of President Bush's successful effort in 2005 to shift jurisdiction over many corporate liability trials to the federal level, considered far less receptive to citizen's suits than state courts. In 2004 and 2005, according to 990 forms filed with the Internal Revenue Service, the company's foundation, the Procter & Gamble Fund, donated at least $90,000 to three conservative legal institutions and think tanks—the National Legal Center, Washington Legal Foundation, and the Reason Foundation—that are leading advocates for tort reform and provide background research for the Chamber of Commerce's rollback efforts.[30]

Thus, tort reformers get it both ways: arguing that more rigorous regulation of chemicals is not necessary because America's punitive civil justice system will take care of abuses, while at the same time using financial and logistical resources to undermine that very system.

There could, however, be unexpected consequences in the courtroom from the legal torque that is emerging over differing international safety standards. One of the central issues to be proven in a product liability case is, could a product have been designed more safely, with less destructive effect on its user? The changes in Europe are suggesting a new means of answering that question.

Derek Johnson, president of the Oregon Trial Lawyers Association, steered me to a case in 2005 that he and his fellow product liability attorneys followed with considerable interest, one involving an unrelated product: automobiles. More than a thousand lawsuits were filed against the Ford Motor Company in state courts on behalf of car-accident victims who were killed or injured after the roof in the company's Explorer SUV collapsed. The company has thus far had to pay more than $150 million in damages to victims and their families. Key to their winning evidence, according to explanations by attorneys on the cases reported in the *Detroit News*, has been evidence gathered from roof tests conducted by Ford's wholly owned European car company, Volvo.[31] That manufacturer was making roofs on comparable cars in Sweden that withstood the impacts from collisions that were killing or injuring American passengers. Could a product have been "designed more safely"? One factor in the successful lawsuits, according to Derek Johnson, was the juries' acceptance that Ford's own Swedish subsidiary was designing roofs more safely.

This principle has yet to be applied to cosmetics. However, for companies facing conflicting standards of safety across the economic spectrum, the liability stakes are being heightened. "That standard of proof could get easier to argue to a jury if you have one product produced here, and the same or similar product produced in Europe or somewhere with higher safety standards," commented Johnson.[32] Judgments like the one which awarded $2.9 million to a Seattle woman scorched by a hot cup of McDonald's coffee, are cited by tort reform advocates as the types of "frivolous litigation" they hope to staunch. But such cases are relatively rare, argues David Wirth, professor of international law at Boston University. If Americans lose their access to the courts, he says, they could "end up with neither strong regulation nor the legal correctives offered by the tort system. . . . The occasional excesses of tort judgments seem a small price to pay for the important backstop provided by civil liability law."[33]

Companies like Procter & Gamble, straddling the world, now face for the first time in their history a choice, as do American consumers. What to do when a system partly of its own making is outpaced by a system demanding access, and action, on knowledge tucked deeply inside the vaults of corporate confidentiality? Today, the world's largest economy says that some ingredients in cosmetics are not safe enough to be used by human beings; countering that, many of America's largest cosmetic producers say they are. America's federal government, other than its implicit endorsement of the industry's position, is not part of the debate.

This brings us to the heart of the matter, that great organizing principle of our enlightened democracies: science. That malevolent wild tiger (in the Europeans' view) or that harmless caged tiger (in the Americans' view) will recur as we travel the fault lines between the United States and Europe over the precautionary principle—distinctions that are helping reshape production decisions in the global economy. We shall see next what happens when two dueling interpretations of scientific data rise to the center of the ongoing challenge to U.S. primacy now being posed by the European Union.

3

Sex & Plastic

Many things have to happen on a boy's path toward manhood. Foremost among them are a sequence of explosive hormonal releases that begin in utero and continue in the first year after birth. During this time, an infant's metabolic moving parts are running at full speed; the hormones surging into a boy's brain will play a major role in determining everything from gender-based behavior to sex drive to what his sperm count will be twenty years later.

Scientists are coming to understand more thoroughly this growth into maleness by identifying how it may go wrong. A growing number suspect that one way to throw the process askew, is by exposure to a family of polyvinyl-chloride plastic softeners called phthalates (pronounced tha-lates). Phthalates are not integral to the chemical structure of plastic, but are additives, making hard plastic pliable and soft.

In the average home, phthalates are everywhere in shower curtains, shampoo bottles, raincoats, and perfumes (for aiding adherence to the skin). Those plastic rubber ducks floating in the bathtub are so squishy because of the phthalates with which they have been saturated. In hospitals, they are in medical tubing. One of the components of that distinctly "new" smell of a new car comes from phthalates that have been added to the plastic dashboard. The reason that dashboards becomes more brittle as a car grows older is because the phthalates are slowly migrating out and into the interior of the car. When phthalates age, they sweat out of the plastic, and residue enters the air, or— through direct contact—the skin.

For infants, exposure comes through multiple routes: they can take in phthalates while in the womb from their umbilical cord or later from the milk they suck from their mother's breast. Exposure can come from dust in the air, from plasticized wall coverings or flooring, and from decaying resins in plastic containers. It can also come from sucking on plastic toys and teething rings, which phthalates help make supple enough for children to play with or put into their mouths. Indeed, the World Health Organization now says that the interactions between children and their toys put them at the center of a potential "risk triangle." Infants, according to the Intergovernmental Forum on Chemical Safety, an affiliate of the World Health Organization, have far less capacity for detoxifying chemicals than adults, and with toys face all three points of that "triangle": "increased vulnerability" to a chemical's "toxic effects," and plenty of possibilities for exposure through "intimate contact" with toys.[1]

One of the most widely used phthalates is called di(2-ethylhexyl) phthalate, or DEHP. Once ingested or inhaled, DEHP heads straight for the stomach and gets broken down into a metabolite called MEHP that can be absorbed by the cells. This includes the cells of the pituitary gland. The pituitary acts like the conductor of an orchestra, coordinating the activities of glands that release hormones responsible for triggering development of everything from the nervous system to the brain to the testes. Hormones are the body's biochemical messengers between the cells, Fed Ex packets of neurological information for turning on, or turning off, the production of specific physiological, psychological, and sexual characteristics. In the testes that includes testosterone, the primary male sex hormone.

The problem with DEHP is that ingesting it can impede the production of LH, a hormone whose main job is to trigger cells in the testes—the Leydig cells—to produce testosterone. How that happens is not yet clear, but what is clear is that when DEHP enters the pituitary, LH levels drop, and a cascade of effects follows. Lower levels of LH traveling to the testes mean less stimulation to the Leydig cells, and testosterone levels plummet. Sexual malformations may follow.

This description of DEHP's effects on the developing male infant is drawn from research by, and interviews with, two of America's leading scientists on the physiological effects of chemical exposure: Dr. Shanna Swan, director of the Center for Reproductive Epidemiology at the University of Rochester School of Medicine and Dentistry in New York, who's been studying the effect of chemicals on the reproductive system for more than a decade; and Dr. Earl Gray, who has been studying the effect of endocrine-disrupting chemicals on rodents for seventeen years at the Environmental Protection Agency's research facility in Research Triangle Park, North Carolina.

Dr. Gray was the scientist who first identified the key hormonal stimulant to sexual development in mice. In research conducted for the Department of Health Services' Center for the Evaluation of Risks to Human Reproduction (CERHR), Dr. Gray reported that female rats fed phthalates during pregnancy gave birth to a significantly high rate of male pups with incompletely descended testes and with an otherwise rare condition known as hypospadias—in layman's terms, an opening of the penis elsewhere than on the tip of the shaft.[2] Both are symptoms of lower than normal testosterone. Scientists, Gray said, had begun calling the deformations they were seeing in the reproductive systems of male mice the "phthalate syndrome," including lower testosterone levels, altered growth of the testes, and lower sperm counts. Dr. Gray told me that he is concerned about what appear to be parallels emerging in the response to phthalates by infant male mice and infant human boys.[3]

Dr. Shanna Swan authored a study, published in August 2005 in the scientific journal *Environmental Health Perspectives* that sent shock waves through the medical community. Swan took urine samples from 134 pregnant women in three cities—Los Angeles, California, Minneapolis, Minnesota, and Columbia, Missouri—and tested them for phthalate levels. The results showed an apparent correlation between women who had higher phthalate levels in their urine and their male children who, within thirteen months of birth, showed "reduced ano-genital distance." That measurement between the anus and the scrotum, known as AGD, is a means of distinguishing the difference between male and female in rodents and is a key indicator of testosterone levels. Dr. Gray has been seeing shorter AGDs in rats fed phthalates; now Dr. Swan was seeing it in infant humans. In baby boys, Swan wrote, "The association between male genital development and phthalate exposure is consistent with the phthalate-related syndrome of incomplete virillization that has been reported in pre-natally exposed rodents."[4] Phthalates, it seems, decrease the development of androgens, one of the hormones critical to sexual development.

On January 10, 2006, I sat in a hearing room in the California state capitol in Sacramento as Dr. Gray and Dr. Swan presented these and other revelations to the health committee of the state assembly. They had been called in to testify by Democratic assemblywoman Wilma Chan, who authored a bill to ban DEHP and five other phthalates from use in toys "intended to be mouthed by children under three years of age." Chan's bill also proposed the banning of bisphenol A (BPA) from toys; another plastic additive—this one makes plastic more rigid and unbreakable—BPA has been linked to the development of prostate and breast cancer in adults. Most of the scientists' attention that day was focused on DEHP, one of the most heavily studied of all the phthalates used by the plastics industry.

The chamber was packed with legislative aides, lobbyists, and environmental-health activists. Nine months earlier, a Harvard School of Public Health study had revealed alarming levels of DEHP in the urine of babies in two Boston intensive-care hospitals, who were being exposed through the plastic tubing and bags used for intravenous fluids.[5] At the end of 2006, the National Toxicology Program in the National Institute of Environmental Health Sciences concluded that the risks from DEHP exposure from medical devices had reached the highest levels of scientific apprehension—known in the toxicological trades as "serious concern." "There is serious concern," states the National Toxicology Program assessment, "that certain medical treatments of male infants may result in DEHP exposure levels that adversely affect development of the male reproductive tract."[6] The Food and Drug Administration had even recommended that hospitals not use intravenous tubes made with phthalates for sensitive pediatric operations or on pregnant women.[7] But that recommendation came with no teeth. The American Nurses Association had subsequently launched an effort to convince the FDA to, at a minimum, require labeling of intravenous tubes and other medical equipment containing DEHP so doctors can avoid using them on children.[8]

On that day in Sacramento, however, the discussion was about toys as a source of otherwise healthy infants' exposure to phthalates. Assemblywoman Chan wanted them removed from products that "are accessed by our most vulnerable population, young children."

Dr. Gray shared his concerns with the panel, that declining sperm counts among American men and the rising incidence of unusual conditions, like hypospadias and testes cancer, suggest the possible outcome of early phthalate exposure. "The research," he said, "suggests more and more concern about phthalates."

Dr. Swan condensed the findings of her tests on pregnant women and their male offspring into layman's terms for the committee: "Wherever we've looked," she said, "human studies are consistent with rodent studies. Phthalates are making the ano-genital distance shorter, in a more feminine direction."

When I called her after the hearing, Dr. Swan said that one of her greatest concerns was that the constraints to testosterone development were occurring in the first three to twelve months of life, a period when boys normally experience a surge of hormone releases that approximates that of puberty. Swan said she hoped to follow up with the children in her study to assess whether such physiological alterations provoke changing patterns in gender-based behavior. Such changes have already appeared in rodents fed anti-androgenic chemicals, like phthalates. She fears that phthalates may be partly responsible for "the feminization of infant boys."[9]

This was pretty strong language from two of America's most eminent specialists on the developing endocrine system. It certainly caught my attention. But in science, of course, nothing is ever clear-cut. Forests get clear-cut, scientific conclusions are rarely so. Decisiveness is rare in science, where one finding is as likely to raise further questions as it is to resolve others.

At the health committee hearing, representatives from the chemical and toy industries challenged Swan and Gray's findings. It is not a question, they argued, that phthalates can cause problems at levels to which they've been fed to rodents. It is a question of how much, when, and how they're exposed to human beings.

Dr. James Lamb, a former EPA reproductive biologist now working for the Weinberg Group, a consulting firm that lobbies on behalf of the chemical industry, asserted that the effects seen in animals from phthalate exposure were from quantities placed in their feed that had no corollary to the exposure of children playing with or sucking on toys. "Phthalate syndrome," he said, "is a rat syndrome, not a human syndrome."

Lamb claimed that Swan's findings did not include other variables in the mother's genetics that could be influencing the symptoms she was seeing in their children, nor lifestyle questions, such as alcohol consumption. Lamb encouraged the lawmakers to review critiques of Swan's work on the Web site of the Phthalate Esthers Panel, which is supported by a consortium of plastics manufacturers and the American Chemical Council, the chemical industry trade association.[10] The primary challenge to Swan's work on that site is contained in a letter to *Environmental Health Perspectives* from the heads of the cosmetic-industry trade associations in the United States and Europe, and a report by the National Institutes of Health questioning whether her use of AGD as a marker for infant health was too new to the field of studying sexual development to be scientifically significant.

Representing the toy companies, Joan Lawrence, the vice president for Standards and Regulatory Affairs of the Toy Industry Association, assured the panel that, "If there was solid scientific evidence that these products were harmful, the toy industry would be the first to remove them." In the corridor after the hearing, Ms. Lawrence expressed to me her impatience with a topic that for toy manufacturers cuts close to home: "Look, I've been in the toy industry for fourteen years. Most important, I'm a mother. I have three kids. They're my main concern, and I'm confident: the toys my kids play with are safe. Safety is the highest priority for the toy industry. Don't forget, manufacturers give those toys to their kids too!"[11]

The question that Ms. Lawrence and Dr. Lamb posed to the committee was this: Had Drs. Swan and Gray and other scientists established a link between phthalates and sexual malformation beyond a shadow of a doubt? The answer, Drs. Gray and Swan conceded, was no. The link, they agreed, between infant phthalate exposure and the symptoms of endocrine disruption are highly suggestive, but have yet to be definitively proven.

None of the advocates for Assemblywoman Chan's proposed ban argued that the amount of phthalates to which an infant would be exposed by toys alone would be enough to trigger the spiral of dysfunction prompted by lower levels of testosterone. Nor could they say with absolute certainty that phthalates were the cause of the troubles they were seeing. But the risks of doing nothing, they said, were far greater than the risks of doing something, even in the face of uncertainty.

Removing phthalates from children's toys, the scientists told the panel, would make for one less contaminant amid multiple exposures to phthalates and other endocrine-disrupting chemicals through infancy and into adulthood. It would reduce at least one possible contributor to rising endocrine-related troubles, and sexual dysfunction levels, in American men. The argument is similar concerning cosmetics: one chemical in one product may have minimal effect, but at a time when humans are exposed to chemicals of every description, quantities rise from multiple sources. Risks from the as yet little understood mixing of all those different substances together are heightened. "We must think in terms of the accumulation of chemicals," asserted Swan. "Not one chemical alone, but how they interplay with the multiplicity of other chemicals." At a minimum, Chan and her panel of scientists argued, eliminating DEHP and other phthalates from toys would remove at least one potential cause of these conditions.

In doing so, they had a model to fall back on: the European Union.

The debate that played out in Sacramento in the winter of 2006 had been settled in the waning days of the twentieth century in Europe. The EU mandated precisely what Joan Lawrence had said the toy industry would do if presented with convincing evidence. It took phthalates out of young children's toys back in 1999.

Over the last ten years, numerous studies on phthalates' effects on human beings were published in European scientific journals. In the Netherlands, scientists asked grown men to chew on pieces of plastic children's toys, then tested their saliva and blood and concluded how easily phthalates pass into the human body;[12] in Denmark, scientists concluded that high levels of phthalates in mother's breast milk contributed to lower levels of testosterone in their male offspring in their first three months of life;[13] and in Italy, doctors reported that phthalates could contribute to premature births.[14] In 1998, the European Chemicals Bureau, an arm of the European Commission that reviews research on chemical toxicity, affirmed that phthalates slough easily off products like plastic toys, and recommended that the commission establish tighter exposure standards.[15] Across Europe, parents expressed alarm: If these were really such powerful endocrine disrupters, as scientists are suggesting they could be, what are they doing in my son's crib? (In children, the evidence then and now has suggested disruptive effects on testosterone levels, thus most concern has been focused on infant boys.)

Responding to mounting public fears in 1999, the EU issued a temporary ban on the inclusion of six phthalates in children's "toys and teethers intended to be mouthed by children under three years of age." The ban was renewed yearly, as scientists were encouraged to get to the heart of these concerns. The World Wildlife Fund took blood samples from members of the European Parliament in 2004 and detected phthalates in all thirty-nine of the MEPs tested.[16] A year later the parliament voted overwhelmingly to make the temporary ban permanent.

As of January 2007, three phthalates determined to be reproductive toxins—DEHP and two others, DBP and BBP—have been banned from "all toys and childcare articles." Three others deemed to be less dangerous—DINP, DIDP, and DNOP—are banned from toys, "if those articles can be put into the mouth by children."[17] The bans are in place until 2010, when they will be put up for review or renewal, depending on the results of continuing scientific research. In a press release, the parliament declared: "Toys and childcare articles which, although not intended for that purpose, can be put in the mouth, may under certain circumstances present a risk to the health of small children if they are made of plasticized material, or include

parts made of plasticized material, which contains certain phthalates." Some EU member countries, like Austria and Germany,
imposed even tighter restrictions on phthalates, limiting their use in
the plastic wrapping that comes in contact with food. An EU risk
assessment classifies DEHP as a danger to adults as well as children,
concluding that the substance "should be regarded as if [it] impair[s]
fertility in humans" and "should be regarded as if [it] causes developmental toxicity to humans."[18] For those reasons, it also falls under
the Cosmetics Directive, which requires that DEHP and other
phthalates be removed from cosmetics and other personal-care products because they have been identified as a contributor to lower
sperm counts in adult males, and a possible carcinogen in both men
and women.

The European Union chose to act even though the direst fears
about the physiological effects of phthalates have yet to be definitively proven. But in the face of a growing body of evidence that
phthalates could be causing serious damage to children's developing
endocrine systems, the EU determined that action was warranted.
The language of the European directive makes that reliance explicit:
"The precautionary principle," it reads, "should be applied where
scientific evaluation does not allow the risk to be determined with
sufficient certainty in order to ensure a high level of protection of
health, in particular for children." This presumption holds that the
risks of not acting on potential chemical poisons outweigh the risks
of acting, even in the face of scientific uncertainty.

In doing so, the Europeans are facing head-on an intensifying
conundrum in the field of toxic epidemiology, which has been made
far more complicated by the abundance of possible contaminants
unearthed by scientists and environmental-health advocates over the
past two decades. Is it, for example, the lead or the mercury that has
led to declining IQs in children living in highly industrialized areas?
Is it the benzene or the PCBs or any number of other carcinogens
that contribute to cancer clusters? Or is it, as industry argues, a

genetic predisposition or lifestyle factors such as drug or alcohol consumption that are the most significant contributing factors? Given
the multiplicity of potential exposure sources and the elongated time
frames in which they happen—over months, years, or decades—set-
tling such question with finality will always be elusive. While U.S.
regulators are impelled to seek a scientifically improbable smoking
gun—evidence that comes when disaster actually strikes—their
European counterparts act on the principle of preventing harm
before it happens, even in the face of scientific uncertainty. In other
words, explained Robert Donkers, the EU's environment counselor
in Washington, D.C., the EU acts on the basis of "precaution."
"Unlike in the United States, we don't wait until we have 100 percent proof," Donkers comments. "Rather, if there's fear, scientific
suspicions, that [a chemical] could cause irreversible damage in the
future, we don't want to wait. By the time it's [definitively] proven, it
could be much too late to do anything about it."

Many other countries are following the Europeans' lead,
including Japan, Norway, Argentina, and Mexico—which have
banned DEHP and other phthalates from most infant toys—and
others, like Canada, which have banned them in teethers and baby
rattles. That leaves the United States as one of the few developed
countries with no government limits on phthalates in toys aimed at
young children.

Ironically, the European Union's decision was based to a significant
degree on evidence generated by American scientists, much of it
funded by the U.S. government. Dr. Gray, for example, works for the
EPA. The EPA has also funded many other American scientists'
research on phthalates, including that of Dr. Swan at the University
of Rochester. Both American scientists' findings were ultimately an
important part of the evidentiary foundation of international research
that was used to support the Europeans' decision to limit infants'
phthalate exposure. In fact, a two-hundred-page risk assessment of

DEHP by the National Institute of Environmental Health Sciences' National Toxicology Program was forwarded to the Health and Consumer Protection Directorate in Brussels before it was published in the United States in November 2005, according to Dr. Gray. That assessment concluded that DEHP "may adversely affect male reproductive-tract development if exposures are sufficiently high."[19] Hearings on phthalates were held in the European Parliament, where reference was made to Dr. Gray's and Dr. Swan's work.

That same data, however, has had an entirely different reception in the United States, where phthalates are under no restrictions. The California hearing was the first of its kind anywhere in the country. Both Dr. Gray and Dr. Swan told me that they had never before presented their findings on phthalates to any U.S. legislative body, on either the federal or state level. "Nobody's ever asked," said Dr. Swan.[20]

Phthalates are, it turns out, one of the most heavily studied plastics, and provide a clear example of how different the European and U.S. regulatory approach is when it comes to action on toxic chemicals. U.S. officials have had access to the same data, the same scientists, and the same scientific journals in deciding not to act, that the Europeans have had in deciding to take the opposite course.

Studies date back decades, to at least 1971, when NASA declared that they wanted phthalate-free plastics in the living area of the astronauts they were sending into orbit, after determining that the substance becomes more volatile in space.[21] In 2003, the Harvard School of Public Health reported a correlation between phthalate levels and sperm motility and concentration: the higher the former, the slower and lower the latter.[22] By 2005, the Center for the Evaluation of Risks to Human Reproduction concluded that it had "concern that DEHP exposure can adversely affect reproductive development in infants less than one year old because of their greater susceptibility and uncertainties regarding exposure."[23] The Centers for Disease Control's ongoing assessment of chemicals in the human body found phthalates in every one of its most recent test subjects; almost without exception, the highest levels were among women and children, those most vulnerable to passing along, or experiencing, its endocrine-disrupting effects.[24] The National Toxicology Program also stated that it had "concern"—the second highest level of apprehension—over "the effects of DEHP exposure on development of the male reproductive tract for infants less than one year old. Diet, mouthing of DEHP-containing objects and certain medical treatments may lead to DEHP exposures that are higher than those experienced by the general population."[25]

But the research conducted by American scientists on phthalates has had nowhere to land in the U.S. regulatory universe, and so has been shot straight over the head of Washington to Brussels. There, the willingness to make a decision based on what will always be partial information if the risks are great enough, strikes at the central difference between the U.S. and European approach to chemicals. Facing the evidence of potential damage to male infants, the European Union determined that action was warranted. Awaiting further definitive confirmation of the links between phthalate exposure and endocrine troubles in infants years later, the United States government has opted not to act.

Jurisdiction over phthalates in the United States is scattered: the EPA has responsibility for phthalates released into the environment; the FDA for medical devices like intravenous tubes; the National Institutes of Occupational Safety and Health for workplace exposure (there appear to be higher pancreatic cancer rates among phthalate workers).[26] In each agency, U.S. policy makers are confronted with a powerful industry lobby that has largely succeeded in shaping a regulatory culture that imposes an obstacle course of cost-benefit analyses before acting.

"If you're a U.S. regulator, it's hard to resist the culture of analysis paralysis," says Joel Tickner, a toxicologist at the Lowell Center for Sustainable Production at the University of Massachusetts. "The more we think we don't know, the less the imperative to act."[27]

The one body with explicit jurisdiction over toys is the Consumer Products Safety Commission (CPSC). In 1998, a petition was submitted to the commission by a coalition of environmental-health groups—including the National Environmental Trust, the Science and Environmental Health Network, and Greenpeace—demanding a ban on polyvinyl chloride, which contains phthalates, in children's toys. The CPSC went on to review industry toxicity studies of DINP, a phthalate that is similar to DEHP, and then in 2003 conducted a study of children's interactions with plastic toys. The CPSC's Human Relevance Working Group, the team charged with assessing people's interactions with potentially dangerous products, installed a set of video cameras to monitor the "mouthing behavior" of 169 children in Houston and Chicago for two days. Another 491 children were observed by their parents or legal guardians who were asked to take notes as to their children's behavior. In both phases, the frequency the children (55 percent boys, 45 percent girls) mouthed soft plastic toys spread liberally around them was registered and timed. The results are now commonly referred to in shorthand as the "Kids Suck" study. The Commission concluded that children between three months and three years old spend from 37 to 70 minutes each day engaged in "mouthing" behavior—the time decreasing as the child grows older. The Commission then estimated that the average time spent sucking on plastic items—other than pacifiers—which might contain phthalates amounted to less than 2 minutes for each age group—1.3 minutes for children under one year, 1.9 minutes for children aged 1–2, and 0.8 minutes for 2–3 year olds. This was not enough time spent sucking, the commission concluded, to deliver a "designated health risk" to children under the age of five.[28]

"The dose makes the poison," CPSC spokesman Scott Wolfson explained to me. "There were not enough phthalates released in those toys to pose any danger."[29] Wolfson's comment revealed another of the key differences between the European and American approaches to regulating chemical exposure. In the case of phthalates, the United

States looked at the time that children may be exposed to a potential toxin, in isolation from other sources of exposure, and determined it was not long enough to cause concern. The Europeans looked at phthalates' inherently toxic properties, and decided to limit one potential route of exposure, in this case via toys.

What has been the effect of removing toys with phthalates from the playrooms of European infants? Did European children suddenly find themselves without toys to amuse them? While U.S. government officials were studying videotapes of children sucking on plastic, the EU's "temporary" ban had already been in place for four years. Many alternatives already exist for phthalates; new ones are also being found.

A Danish company, Danisco, one of the largest manufacturers of food additives in the world, introduced a phthalate alternative for toys and other products that has been approved for use in both Europe and the United States. In January 2006, the European Council for Plasticisers and Intermediates participated in a conference, "Plasticisers 2006," that was specifically tailored to encourage the industry to develop phthalate alternatives in response to "increasingly stringent" legislative demands "and environmental awareness among the general population."[30] On the other side of the Atlantic, however, the U.S. plastics industry, represented by the American Chemical Council and other trade associations, is continuing to fight legislative measures like the one in California to restrict their use.

The German chemical giant BASF shut down its European DEHP production after the EU ban in 2005. The company, one of four major global producers, was formerly responsible for half of the phthalates produced in Europe, but "discontinued production of DEHP [in Europe] because the market has changed considerably over the last years," according to William Pagano, a BASF communications officer who responded to my questions in an e-mail. Instead, BASF now has a new and profitable plasticizer line called DINCH. Pagano said the company has spent "five million euros . . . for rigorous and extensive" safety testing of DINCH, and that it has an "outstanding toxicological profile" for "sensitive applications . . . such as toys, food-contact materials, and medical applications." In the United States, however, the company continues to manufacture DEHP at two facilities, in Pittsburgh, Pennsylvania, and Texas City, Texas, for many industrial and consumer-product uses on the American market.[31]

The phthalate ban in Europe had nothing close to the devastating impacts predicted by the global toy industry during parliamentary debates each year over renewing the temporary ban. From 2002 to 2004, European toy-industry sales grew by 5 percent, to nearly twenty billion dollars annually, according to the trade group Toy Industries of Europe.[32] During a comparable period in the United States, from 1999 to 2005, U.S. companies' toy exports to Europe's biggest national markets rose by 3 percent, to $134 million in 2005, according to the U.S. Commerce Department.[33]

I had trouble finding a toy-industry analyst anywhere who said that the phthalate ban had even a "negligible" financial impact on the toy industry. "While I'm aware of different approaches to regulation . . . the subject [of the phthalate ban] almost never comes up on Wall Street," commented John Taylor, managing director of Arcadia Investment Company, which specializes in toys and video-game investments, in an e-mail exchange with my research intern Samuel Schramski. "My sense is that this really isn't an issue."[34] Four analysts we spoke with, including Taylor, had to be reminded that the ban was in place at all; multiple other factors, such as foreign competition and changing children's (and parents') taste, were topmost on their list of concerns.

Eighty-five percent of the world's toys are manufactured in neither Europe nor America, but in China. The remaining 10 percent or so are manufactured in Taiwan, Japan, or the Philippines; only a very few specialty, high-end toys are actually manufactured in either the United States or Europe. Toy companies are really little more than "sales and marketing platforms," said a toy-industry analyst I spoke with. "They don't manufacture anything." The creation of toys is outsourced. So whatever the proscriptions of American or European law, the message must be communicated by the mother companies to their manufacturers abroad, some of which may even be in the same city in China. "It's pretty simple," the analyst said. "Some of those manufacturers [in China] produce toys with phthalates, for the United States and elsewhere, and others produce them without, for Europe and other jurisdictions that ban them." So it's up to the toy companies to determine whose standards they abide by; manufacturers in China and elsewhere have shown they can produce for either market.[35]

Most important, European toy companies have had eight years to make the adjustment to phthalate-free toys, and they have done so. Visit any new mother or father indulging their new infant son in Europe, and you'll see the same goofy animals, same dangling colors and shapes, same dolls and funny plastic-lined books lying around, that you'd see in the home of their American counterpart. The only substantive difference is that a European parent may assume that her child's playthings are not as dangerous to suck on as the playthings in her peer's home across the Atlantic might be. And the curious thing is, even without phthalates, many of those little infant doodads and playful chazerai are plenty pliable.

Dr. Swan told me that what disturbs her most about the ongoing debate over phthalates in America, is that substitutes are working. Why take the risk? Some substances, like DDT, she said, "raise difficult and complicated questions." There may be no alternatives for fighting the mosquitoes that carry malaria than with that infamously toxic pesticide. "There is a real risk-benefit calculus there, because malaria is coming back and DDT may be the most effective way to control it. That risk-benefit is real. But with phthalates you don't have that same calculus. There are alternatives. We can switch. It's doable. Why put this into kids' bodies if we don't have to?"[36]

The toy industry was perhaps the first in the United States to awaken to the rising power of the European Union. In the late nineties, the EU was fifteen countries, with a fraction of the political power it wields today. The aborted General Electric–Honeywell merger was several years away. On the diplomatic front, the United States was leading Europe into a war in its own backyard, in the Balkans—a far different dynamic than would unfold four years later in Iraq. Most American companies didn't think twice about that distant bureaucracy in Brussels. Yet the toy manufacturers saw early what was coming: they saw instinctively how the Europeans' action on phthalates could ripple rapidly across the Atlantic.

The U.S. toy industry enlisted the Clinton administration to lobby on its behalf when the Europeans began questioning phthalate's health effects and reconsidering their status in the late 1990s, and came close to succeeding. Clinton administration officials in the Commerce and State departments wrote letters to their counterparts in Brussels on behalf of the Toy Industry of America (TIA), arguing that the evidence was insufficient to warrant restrictions on phthalates being considered by the EU at that time. In early 1998, a senior vice president of Mattel sent then secretary of commerce William Daley a letter of thanks, obtained through the Freedom of Information Act by the Environmental Health Network, for his assistance in "helping the U.S. toy industry defend against recent EU initiatives to ban the use of polyvinyl chloride (PVC) in toys."[37] European Union action was delayed by a year.

But then a rare thing in the annals of industry-governement relations happened: the Clinton administration reversed course. In a letter to Representative Henry Waxman, who had criticized the administration's efforts "to dissuade other nations from taking precautionary steps against the risk of phthalates," Vice President Al Gore withdrew support from the toy industry's position. "The President and I," Gore wrote on December 21, 1998, "have made it clear that the Departments of Commerce and State should refrain from any actions to discourage individual countries, whether in the European Union or elsewhere, from implementing precautionary measures they deem appropriate to restrict the marketing or use of products containing phthalates." He declared that further research and testing into "potential cancer and endocrine effects of phthalates" would henceforth be given "high priority."[38] Within a year, the EU passed its temporary ban on phthalates, and the Clinton administration initiated a new wave of research directed particularly at the vulnerability of children to phthalates. A year after that, George Bush was elected president. Earl Gray and other scientists had their mandate, but no one to talk to in the government.

When their lobbying campaign failed, the industry giants Mattel and Hasbro, each with significant European sales, announced that they would abide by the European standards and remove phthalates from their worldwide production of toys aimed at young children. Defeated at lobbying in the foreign terrain of Brussels, multinational toy companies would be the first large U.S. firms to follow Europe's tougher standards for protecting environmental health. "TIA members that sell to Europe comply with the Europeans' directive," said Joan Lawrence when I contacted her after the hearing in Sacramento.[39]

The big retailer Toys "R" Us announced shortly after the Europeans' first phthalate moratorium that it would no longer sell toys containing phthalates from all of its stores—they leveraged their standards up globally to meet those of the European Union. Toys "R" Us has 650 outlets in Europe, Asia, and elsewhere around the world, in addition to its nearly 600 stores in the United States. The company's desire to maintain an international market offered a powerful incentive to meet the European standards that it now applies in the United States and other countries.

But those decisions mean little to the legions of manufacturing firms in China and elsewhere that do not sell their toys to Europe, and for whom the United States remains a huge and unregulated market. Company members of the Toy Industry of America, Joan Lawrence told me, agreed "voluntarily" to take DEHP and other phthalates out of rattlers, pacifiers, and teethers, products "intended to be used in the mouth." That agreement was in the 1980s, after concerns surfaced over phthalate's potential carcinogenicity. It did not, however, cover toys. So while transnational companies can demand that their manufacturers in China build phthalate-free toys, companies selling only in the United States are under no pressure to do the same. The result can be seen in the playrooms of American infants.

The non-governmental organizations Environment California and the Public Interest Research Group (PIRG) teamed up to conduct chemical analyses of infant playthings, an exercise never engaged in by the U.S. government. The groups bought teethers, bath books, and toys and sent them to an EPA-certified chemical lab in Chicago for a chemical breakdown. Fifteen of the eighteen products tested contained one or another of the six phthalates now banned in the European Union. A dozen infant products—including waterproof books and bath toys—contained measurable levels of DEHP. [see list of products/companies in graph or in appendix]. Nine of those contained multiple phthalates that toy manufacturers have, at one point or another in the past decade, said they would voluntarily remove. One teether—the Teething Ring, which helps induce infants to suck on oral pain-relief gel inside—contained DEHP. Another, charmingly named the Baby Gund Jungle Collection Teether, contained DBP, a phthalate classified by the EU as a reproductive toxin and carcinogen.[40]

Today, an American who wants phthalate-free toys can find them in the brand names manufactured by multinationals, which have been impelled to remove them by the European Union. Those companies, according to Joan Lawrence, account for about 40 percent of the U.S. market. But for those who do not have the resources, who are more inclined to buy their toys at discount parlors or buy generic brands online—from outlets that sell millions of baby products each year—if the toys are plastic and soft there is a good chance they contain phthalates. There is no way to know for sure if toys do not contain phthalates, short of sending them to a testing laboratory, an investment of thousands of dollars, which makes it a rather implausible option.

This was a breach that Wilma Chan wanted to fill, in her fight for an enforceable ban in Sacramento—and it had all the signs of a replay of the Europeans' struggle seven years earlier. Chan's bill was modeled explicitly on Europe's law; it was, commented Peter Price, a lobbyist representing advocates for the bill, "the EU directive coming to Sacramento."[41] The arguments were the same as had been pushed in Europe, and the key players were the same too. The TIA's members which export to Europe—Mattel and Hasbro are the largest—had finally acceded to the EU's demands to remove phthalates from their infant toys, but back home the trade group launched a lobbying campaign against the effort to impose the same restrictions in California. The Weinburg Group's Brussels-based lobbyists had been a leading voice of U.S. industry opposition to the EU's phthalate initiatives, and would later send its vice president for Applied Toxicology and Risk Sciences, Dr. Jim Lamb, to represent them in Sacramento.[42] Like many U.S. industries, the Weinburg Group is experiencing the unsettled tensions between Europe and America's conflicting standards. "When I was at EPA," Lamb told me, "the Europeans were following what the United States was doing. Now, it's becoming more and more the precautionary principle over there. . . . That has caused great confusion here as to what this means for the United States."[43]

A fundamental and simple question lies just under the surface of transatlantic disputes over the precautionary principle: Is it feasible? Can industry accommodate the demands of public health advocates who argue that a substance be discontinued despite the absence of full scientific consensus—a rare phenomenon—about its toxicity? In Brussels, I interviewed David Cadogan, a chemist who works as the senior scientist for the European Chemical Industry Council (CEFIC), which is Europe's chemical-industry trade group. Before coming to CEFIC, Cadogan spent two decades in the private sector, specializing in the manufacture of plastics, including many phthalates. Now, as a representative of his industry, he had lobbied the parliament against the phthalate ban. He is no fan of the precautionary principle. "The EU," Dr. Cadogan told me, "looked at scientific opinions that created doubts about safety, and made a political decision to ban them." That decision, he said, was prompted by "politicians' desire to appear to be protecting their constituents from scientifically unproven risks." Cadogan conceded, however, that since the ban took effect, it has had little long-term impact on European toymakers. "I suppose in the end," he shrugged, "we've learned to live without it."[44]

Phthalates may have been removed from European toys, but in the United States the industry saw the California proposal as a showdown: If the country's most populous state went on the record saying phthalates are dangerous, then what's a jury going to think if anyone ever decides to sue for health damages five or ten years from now? And what will the rest of the country do when the largest single state market banned a chemical used in toys for sale across the country? After heavy lobbying by the toy and plastics industry, Chan's bill went down to defeat by one vote in the state assembly appropriations committee.

I approached Joan Lawrence of the Toy Industry Association after her testimony to the assembly health committee. She had just told the legislators that California stood to lose thousands of toy-industry jobs if Chan's bill was passed. A quarter of the association's five hundred member companies are based in California, she said, and the state represents nearly one third of national toy sales.

Why, I asked, was her industry opposed to a bill that would require in one state what her biggest members have already accomplished in Europe?

"We're just talking about a few multinational companies," she said. "Most of our companies are small and medium-sized. It would be difficult for them. . . . With this bill you could have no plastic toys produced in California."

I asked her for the names of any member companies that had to abandon the European market because of the directive banning phthalates. She couldn't think of any. "Why then," I wanted to know, "would it be so difficult for them to comply with such a law in the United States?"

"Well," she said, "you wouldn't want them to mix up a shipment of American toys with a shipment of European toys, would you?" She laughed, nervously; she was kidding. Needless to say, such mix-ups couldn't even enter the realm of black humor if the United States was abiding by the same restrictions; there would be nothing to mix up.

It turns out such scenarios may not be so far-fetched. Six months after my brief talk with Joan Lawrence, the EU's Health and Consumer Protection Directorate reported that Lithuanian authorities had confiscated a shipment of "squeaky toys in form of a giraffe, a bear, and a beaver," because of their DEHP content. Two weeks later, in July, the Czechs were confiscating a shipment of pillowy "cube(s) that make sounds" because of the presence of two phthalates, DEHP and DINP. Both violated the Toys Directive. Both, according to the Rapid Alert System for Non-Food Products (RAPEX), which tracks compliance with EU safety laws, were manufactured in China. RAPEX is a database maintained by Europe's twenty-five national customs services to monitor imports coming into the EU, and offers an extraordinary ongoing picture, week by week, of the products that are violating EU consumer-protection laws.[45] It is there, at Europe's frontiers, in the customs authorities' warehouses of confiscated goods, where the differences in protection afforded Europeans and Americans come sharply into focus. RAPEX does not list product brand names; it does, though, include a picture of the item in question, and all were taken off the market immediately. There is absolutely nothing to stop those, or any other, confiscated shipments of infant playthings blocked from sale in Europe from being diverted to that other big market across the sea, the United States.

Soon, there was another twist: the city of San Francisco took Chan's idea and passed a municipal ordinance "prohibiting the sale of toys and child-care articles made with phthalates" from being sold within the city limits. That made San Francisco the first government anywhere in the country to take action to limit children's exposure to phthalates. The idea had come direct from Brussels to Sacramento to San Francisco, detouring Washington altogether. As of January 1, 2007, the sellers of toys containing the same six phthalates singled out by the EU, and aimed at children "under the age of three," would be subject to municipal fines that could amount to thousands of dollars. Shortly before the bill took effect, the San Francisco Chronicle tested some randomly purchased toys and discovered that at least three out of sixteen exceeded the city's phthalate limits. Those included a teether, a baby doll, and a rubber ducky—sold at a chain drug store, Walgreen's—which had thirteen times the allowable level of DEHP.[46] The response of industry was not to remove them, but to sue the city. The Toy Industry of America, along with the American Chemistry Council, the California Chamber of Commerce, and local toy stores sued the city to try and block its implementation on the grounds that, on such matters, city law is preempted by the federal consumer Product Safety Commission.[47]

The case was pending as the law took effect in January 2007—when residents of San Francisco became the only Americans in the country who could shop with some level of certainty that the toys purchased for their children would contain no phthalates. For other Americans, though, the choice was not so simple: They'd have to get on an airplane.

By the summer of 2008, as revulsion and impatience with reports of toxic toys grew across the United States, Congress passed a bill into law that tightened the CPSC's surveillance authority and specifically banned the same six phthalates that had been banned nine years earlier from toys in the European Union. San Francisco would no longer be alone. That national ban takes effect on February 10, 2009. One of the last acts, however, of the Bush adminstration's CPSC was to declare that companies may still sell any toys containing phthalates as long as they were manufactured before that date—virtually guaranteeing that toys with phthalates will be around in the United States for some time to come. (In December, the CPSC's decision to permit the sale of toy inventories was challenged in court by two NGOs, the Natural Resource Defense Council and Public Citizen, which argued that, "This will cause direct harm to individuals exposed to these chemicals in children's products and consumer confusion about which products sold in stores comply with the phthalates ban." The groups' demand for an injunction was unresolved as of mid-December.)

The battle over phthalates suggests how the same science can lead to different results. The United States, which once could justifiably presume that others listened when it acted, is discovering that in its regulatory approach to science fewer and fewer are doing so. New forces are emerging, and what once was widely accepted American leadership is starting to seem more and more old-fashioned. U.S. officials have been discovering this, to their surprise, in some of the most unexpected of locales.

4

Two Houses of Risk

It was at a casino-resort complex near the Uruguayan capital of Montevideo, thousands of miles from Brussels or Washington, where the global balancing of power that has governed our chemical era were upended. Little noticed by most Americans, in May 2005 eight hundred delegates from around the world gathered at the Punta del Este resort to discuss the future of some of the most toxic substances on earth.

On the ground floor of the resort was one of Latin America's biggest casinos, where avid gamblers were playing the odds at the poker tables, blessing the dice, taking their chances with the slots. Below the casino, in a complex of ballrooms, the delegates were playing the odds of another sort. Here, in the pungent tropical air of the South Atlantic, the first meeting of the parties that had ratified a global treaty called the Stockholm Convention on Persistent Organic Pollutants, known commonly as POPS, unfolded over four days.

If The Hague had a list of chemical war criminals, the dozen POPS chemicals would be on it, including chlordane, heptachlor, aldrin, dieldrin, mirex, DDT, hexachlorobenzene, toxaphene, polychlorinated biphenyls (PCBs), dioxins, and furans. Twenty years ago the NGO Pesticide Action Network had dubbed these the world's "dirty dozen," and the name had stuck. All act like light switches of toxicity upon the human body—potent neurotoxins and carcinogens that most countries in the world had agreed to kick out of global commerce.

Over half a century, hundreds of millions of tons of these chemicals have been sprayed from nozzles, coated onto seeds, and leaked from factories and waste dumps into the soil and water supply. One of those chemicals, the pesticide DDT, had subsequently wreaked such damage to the ecosystem—wildlife in treated areas began giving birth to mutant offspring—that the biologist Rachel Carson was prompted to write *Silent Spring*, a book that helped trigger the rise of today's environmental movement.

In May 2001, at a meeting in Stockholm, the POPS Treaty was launched when the international community had little trouble agreeing that the poison in those chemicals vastly outweighed whatever benefits they might have once offered to farmers and consumers. By the time of the Montevideo meeting, ninety-eight countries had ratified the POPS Treaty, committing themselves to removing the "dirty dozen" chemicals from international commerce. Signatories ranged from the most developed to the least, from every member state of the European Union to Japan, Australia, Brazil, Mexico, Thailand, Congo, Malawi, Paraguay, and Chad. Richer countries agreed to shoulder most of the fifty million dollars that treaty members would need annually to phase out and dispose of the forbidden chemicals. In Punta del Este, the United States was alone among developed countries in not having ratified the POPS Treaty.[1]

President Bush inherited POPS from the waning days of the Clinton administration and signed it shortly before Earth Day, in April 2001. In a Rose Garden ceremony, he pointed to broad bipartisan support for the treaty and commented that POPS chemicals "respect no boundaries and can harm Americans even when released abroad."[2] Chemicals that had already been banned in the United States, President Bush warned, could come back to Americans in their food; he promised a rapid ratification by the Senate. At first glance, the treaty posed minimal threat to the status quo. In essence, it formalized the elimination of chemicals that had been, for the most part, banned from use in the United States and in Europe for more than a decade. The problem for the Bush administration, however, surfaced quickly: the treaty provides for adding new chemicals to the blacklist if they are shown to have qualities of persistence in the environment, accumulate in human tissues, and are mobile (many of the POPS chemicals have been found in extremely high levels in the blood of indigenous peoples in Alaska and along the Arctic Circle). Chemicals meeting these criteria are subject to review by a panel of scientists selected by the signatory nations. Further bans could be declared; more chemicals could be declared unwanted. POPS was sent into the Washington deep freeze.

Instead of heading to the House to consider modest legal changes to bring U.S. law into conformity with the treaty and then to the Senate for ratification, POPS went to the president's legal team — which began undermining the treaty's rationale before the ink on its boss's signature was dry. From the Office of Legal Counsel in the Justice Department came a gem of pretzel logic that amounted to a head-on challenge to the mainstay principles of international agreements. Assistant Attorney General William Moschella issued an opinion that ratifying POPS would create an international process for restricting chemicals, to which the United States would be bound, compelling action by the executive branch (via the Environmental Protection Agency) and by Congress (via the legal changes required to keep the United States in compliance) that would violate the separation of powers clause of the Constitution.[3] The administration's argument would later be refuted by a

Congressional Research Service analysis, which concluded that POPS could easily "pass constitutional muster."[4] In the Republican congress, however, that didn't help move the treaty off the ice block onto which it had been thrown. That is, until the price of disengagement became clear. As the United States has learned from other international agreements with which it has refused to cooperate, the world kept moving forward without its participation.

The POPS meeting commenced in the cavernous Punta del Este Ballroom, situated just below the thriving casino upstairs. More than fifty rows of chairs filled the room—there sat every country from Australia, Belgium, Brazil, China, Hungary, Japan, Korea, Mexico, Nigeria, Spain, Turkey, all the way down to Zambia. At the back of the room were three rows set aside for "nonvoting observers," including representatives who had not ratified the treaty. There sat three delegates from the U.S. government—two from the EPA and one from the State Department. They found themselves in unusual company. To either side were other nonvoting observers, including NGO representatives from the Center for International Environmental Law and the Pesticide Action Network, both of which had spent years working on behalf of POPS and were highly critical of the EPA, and industry groups like the American Chemical Council, which had spent years fighting against POPS and other environmental initiatives. They had traveled a long way to sit in the same room. All were diplomatically polite with one another. "At gatherings like that," Pesticide Action Network representative Kristin Schafer recalled, "we just agree to vehemently disagree."[5]

Among the EPA's two delegates was Janice Jensen, one of the agency's key point people for keeping pace with environmental initiatives happening around the world. Jensen is director of the Field and External Affairs Division of the EPA's Office of Pesticide Programs, and part of her job involves maintaining ties with international bodies like this one to share the EPA's expertise. The other part of her job involves overseeing what is probably the world's single most significant repository of toxicity data on those POPS chemicals, which her agency has been monitoring for decades. "POPS," she told me, "is the first international treaty [on chemicals] with real teeth and real bucks behind it."[6]

Ms. Jensen found herself in an awkward position: she was U.S. liaison to an agreement her government hadn't ratified, and overseer of a trove of information about chemicals over whose international fate she had no control. A congressional aide who attended POPS negotiations as an observer in Montevideo, and later in Geneva, told me that the United States had so few friends at the meetings that he recalled watching a State Department official being reduced to passing notes about U.S. positions to a delegate from the Congo. His heart sank as he watched one of the world's most troubled and fragile governments speak on behalf of the United States. "When I saw him passing that note to the Congo," the aide recalled, "I knew how far we had fallen."[7]

In diplomatic terms, the United States was about to fall further. On the afternoon of May 5, 2005 Mexico's delegate to POPS, Daniel Chacon Anaya, from that country's health secretariat, rose from the floor. The chair was accepting nominations for the next round of chemicals to be put on the POPS list. Anaya rose to nominate the pesticide lindane, long suspected of carcinogenic and neurotoxic properties, to be added to the POPS list and banned around the world. Lindane is an organochlorine pesticide developed to kill the pests that attack seeds before germination; since the 1940s, when it was introduced, hundreds of millions of pounds have been coated onto seeds before planting in countries around the world. The Mexican delegate's move sent a message that power in POPS would not be limited to the rich, more developed countries.

In their nomination papers, Anaya cited numerous studies,

including those by the EPA, the Extension Service of the U.S.
Department of Agriculture, the International Agency for Research
into Cancer, the World Health Organization, and Mexico's own
National Institute of Ecology, suggesting lindane's toxicity as a dis-
rupter of the liver and the nervous system in animals and as a possible contributor to breast and other cancers in human beings.[8] He
also cited the fifty-two other countries—including the twenty-five
countries of the EU, Russia, Japan, South Africa, New Zealand, and
Canada—that had already banned lindane, and the thirty-three
others that had placed it under severe restriction. In support of
Mexico's action, members of the International POPS Elimination
Network hosted a midday snack, where they served eggs, salmon,
and other dishes, which they revealed contained high levels of lindane and other POPS chemicals. "Global action is needed," Anaya's
plea concluded, "to halt the pollution caused worldwide by lindane
and its production."

Another message went straight to the back of the room, where the
U.S. delegation was seated along with other "observers." "There
wasn't exactly stunned silence," recalled Janice Jensen. "But surprise,
yes." The EPA had two years before completed a reregistration review
process of lindane and had affirmed its registration for use as a seed
treatment for six crops—sorghum, wheat, barley, corn, oats, and rye.[9]
Lindane is also used in medicinal shampoos to kill lice, available in
every state except California, where lindane-based shampoos are
banned. (In 1997, the Food and Drug Administration banned the use
of lindane for veterinary purposes for treatment of lice on animals; for
people, the agency recommends its use for patients who cannot tol-
erate or have failed treatment with safer medication."[10]

For the first time, a developing country—Mexico—was proposing
the ban of a chemical that was approved for use in the land of its
long-dominant, and far richer, northern neighbor. The United States
was being outflanked by a country that had previously been seen

only as a regulatory black hole, at best, and, at worst, the recipient of many chemicals banned in the United States.

The man who wrote the lindane section of Mr. Anaya's presentation was Dr. Mario Yarto, an environmental chemist at the National Ecology Institute, the scientific arm of the Mexican Ministry of Environment and Natural Resources. Yarto, the agency's director of Toxic Chemicals, had spent the previous three years conducting studies on lindane's toxic properties and how it travels through the environment. In Montevideo, he was chief scientific adviser to Mr. Anaya; in 2006, Yarto became Mexico's official delegate to POPS.

I called Dr. Yarto several months after a follow-up POPS meeting in Geneva, in which lindane had been formally accepted for review—the first step toward a global ban. Yarto is a reserved man, a precise talker; he is hardly a fiery eco-radical. His background is in chemistry, and he is not used to making history. He expressed great respect for the data that had been collected by the EPA on lindane, and which was made available to him by Janice Jensen—data that had contributed to Mexico's decision to ban the pesticide, and subsequently to the global community's decision to consider it for worldwide elimination.

But Yarto was also aware, as were many others in the room that day, of the leap into a new era his country's position on lindane represented—particularly in the long-standing reliance Mexico has had on the United States. "Strong differences," he told me, "have emerged between our two countries at this time. If the United States follows policies that do not benefit the environment, then it is Mexico's opportunity to show leadership in terms of environmental decision making."[11]

The Mexican proposal had particular poignancy for Janice Jensen. Six years previously, she had sat with her Mexican and Canadian counterparts at a meeting in Toronto of the Commission on Environmental Cooperation (CEC), which facilitates coordinated environmental strategies among the three partners of the North American Free Trade Agreeement. At that meeting, she and several of her EPA colleagues had proposed that the three countries develop a North American risk assessment plan for lindane—the first step toward tighter restrictions or an outright continental ban on its use. The NAFTA partners agreed; a transnational risk assessment was launched.[12] Lindane's days appeared to be numbered.

Then George Bush was elected president. Lindane assessments were put through what Luke Trip, program manager for the CEC's Sound Management of Chemicals Program, told me were "unprecedented review."[13] A former head of the EPA's Office of Pesticide Programs, Edwin L. Johnson, became the pesticide's chief advocate after leaving the agency to become an industry lobbyist.[14] Progress on the trinational level slowed to a crawl, while American farmers continued to dip their seeds into lindane solution or inject it into the soil.

Mexico, however, forged ahead with the risk assessments and research into alternatives that had been called for by the 1999 agreement. It turned out, Yarto told me, that there were plenty of alternatives—many of them tested in farmlands of Europe, where lindane had been banned from all uses since 2001. "Europe," Yarto commented, "had a long history of finding other ways of controlling those pests."

By September 2004, eight months before the POPS meeting in Montevideo, Yarto himself announced to the startled participants at a CEC meeting in Montreal—with Janice Jensen and other EPA officials attending—that his country was, "not waiting" for the United States. Mexico was banning lindane from all agricultural and pharmaceutical uses as of January 2007.[15] In Punta del Este, Mexico was asking the world to do the same. The United States was alone in its commitment to a chemical on which the rest of the world was rapidly turning its back.

———

Thirty years ago, shortly after the birth of the EPA, the United States began to ban and impose restrictions on the most toxic pesticides and chemicals. One of the major concerns among environmentalists and foreign governments at the time, was whether these new controls would be applied to the export of those products to other countries. Sure enough, they were not. As a young reporter at that time, I coauthored a book with David Weir which revealed that there was indeed a thriving export trade for those banned and restricted chemicals in developing countries. A global double standard was in full bloom. By the millions of gallons these chemicals were exported to countries like Honduras, Peru, India, and indeed, to Mexico. Residues of those banned chemicals ultimately came back to us in the fruits and vegetables the United States imported from those very same countries, which inspired the title of our book, *Circle of Poison*.[16]

But that was then. Mexico's move on lindane revealed how dramatically the global politics around chemicals have changed. When Weir and I wrote our book, we described Mexico as one of the primary markets for pesticides like chlordane, aldrin, dieldrin, and indeed, lindane. Today, it is the United States that is the market for a chemical that is banned in Mexico. The ironies around lindane abound, and offer a snapshot into how profoundly the United States has lost its former position of environmental leadership.

The sole suppliers of lindane since the early part of this century have been the U.S. firm Chemtura, which markets it in bulk, and Gustafson Chemicals, which sells lindane-treated seeds. Gustafson is a Texas-based subsidiary of the multinational chemical and pharmaceutical giant Bayer, headquartered in Germany. Lindane was banned in Germany in 1996 (prior to being banned throughout the EU in 2001). When Weir and I wrote *Circle of Poison* twenty-five years ago, Bayer was one of the companies we identified as selling organochlorine pesticides like aldrin and dieldrin to Mexico and other developing countries, which it couldn't sell in the United

States. Now many of those same chemicals are on the POPS list. In 2005, Bayer voluntarily withdrew lindane from the Mexican market in advance of that country's national ban taking effect. Bayer could not sell lindane on its home turf but it had no problem doing so in the United States. According to a "Lindane Risk Assessment Fact Sheet" issued by the EPA, the amount of lindane applied annually as a seed treatment in the United States was between 65 and 105 tons yearly as of early 2006.[17]

Shortly after Mexico's proposal to nominate lindane in Punta del Este, I spoke with Fernando Bejarano, the director of one of that country's biggest environmental NGOs, the Network for Action on Pesticides and Alternatives in Mexico (RAPAM). Bejarano and RAPAM had played a big role in meeting with Mario Yarto and other government officials to encourage them to rid the country of lindane. Now that they had succeeded, Bejarano told me he had a new concern: that "illicit lindane" would start traveling in the opposite direction of the usual border traffic, "smuggled into Mexico from the USA." Mexico would also have to concern itself with lindane residues coming into their country, just as Americans once had to concern themselves with banned chemical residues coming into the United States on Mexican tomatoes and other crops.[18]

U.S. delegates returned from the POPS meetings in 2005 frustrated over being sidelined from the action. No one had stopped what they were doing because the United States refused to cooperate. Secretary of State Condoleezza Rice started paying attention.

On July 22, Rice and EPA administrator Stephen Johnson wrote a joint letter to then-Senate majority leader Bill Frist that amounted to an admission of how quickly lack of cooperation can turn into lack of power. "In May," Rice and Johnson wrote to Senator Frist, "the U.S. delegation returned from the first POPS Conference of the Parties in Uruguay. Since we were not a party, we failed to obtain membership on an important committee that will review and make recommendations on additional chemicals for future inclusion on the POPS list. The U.S. role in POPS meetings could be further limited if Congress does not act quickly to adopt necessary implementing legislation, compounding the negative repercussions for U.S. leadership in international chemicals fora." She promised—four years after President Bush had signed POPS—the State Department's willingness to "working closely" with Congress to ratify the treaty and make the necessary changes to U.S. law to conform to its requirements.[19]

Within a week, the EPA received notice that lindane's distributors in the United States were "voluntarily withdrawing" their registration for lindane.[20] The same day, July 27, 2006, the EPA announced it was withdrawing lindane registration for all uses in U.S. agriculture.[21] "That's American leadership," quipped Daryl Ditz, who lobbied on behalf of POPS ratification for the Center for International Environmental Law. "That makes the United States the fifty-third country in the world to ban lindane."[22] The EPA's action, however, had no effect on the use of lindane shampoos, which are regulated as a pharmaceutical by the FDA, and still permitted for anti-lice shampoos.

The meeting in Montevideo sent a powerful message home of what can happen when the United States excludes itself from international environmental negotiations. Even the chemical industry began indicating its support for U.S. accession to POPS. Undersecretary of State for Oceans and International Environmental Affairs, Claudia McMurray, was sent to Congress in the spring of 2006 to argue for the urgency of joining the world community and ratifying the treaty. Not doing so, she said, would leave the United States out in the cold as the fate of chemicals was discussed and acted upon by the world community. By this time, two chemically related flame retardants widely used in the United States, penta and octa brominated diphenyl ether (PBDEs), had been proposed to be added to the POPS list. Both are classified by the EPA as possible human carcinogens, and are suspected of disrupting the development of the thyroid gland. They are banned in Europe. In the United States, production is being phased out but they are still being used, and millions of pounds of PBDEs are coated onto electrical appliances, textiles, and packaging, and onto the furnishings in airplanes and trains.[23]

McMurray made a plea to the House Energy and Commerce Committee to permit the country to regain its influence over decisions involving PBDEs and other chemicals. "As the country with the world's most comprehensive risk-management scheme for toxic chemicals," she testified, "the United States should continue its leadership role as an active and influential participant with a seat not just at the table, but at the head of the table."[24]

But the bill supported by the administration to ratify POPS came with a twist. The legal changes proposed by Representative Paul Gillmor, Republican of Ohio, to conform U.S. law with the requirements of the POPS treaty were paired with the elimination of a state's ability to impose more stringent limits on POPS chemicals than those agreed to at the federal level. This amounted to a direct strike at the evolving trend among state governments to fill the void left by the Bush administration's inaction on environmental protection.[25] That includes PBDEs, which have already been banned in several states, including California, Washington, and Maine.

Nor was the U.S. effort to join POPS an altogether welcome development. On the one hand, environmental officials I have spoken to around the world are quick to compliment the technical knowledge and commitment of mid-level EPA officials, whose scientific experience has proved invaluable in understanding the toxicology of chemicals (despite the frequent absence of legal mandates to act on those findings).

But U.S. participation could come with a price. In negotiations, the United States has asked that as a condition for ratifying POPS all votes be by consensus; currently, the treaty requests that parties make "every effort" to adapt "recommendations by consensus," but accepts a two-thirds majority vote if consensus cannot be obtained. Barbara Perthen-Palmisiano, Austria's delegate to POPS, commented to me that U.S. participation would be welcomed with some reservations. Perthen-Palmisiano had worked directly with Mexican agricultural scientists in developing alternatives to lindane as that country launched its effort to remove the substance from Mexican agriculture. "Consensus," she said, "means that nothing can be introduced if the United States is against it."[26]

As the delegates filed out of the Punta del Este ballroom on May 8, they passed through the casino basking in its endless light, abuzz with its whirring slots, bouncing roulette balls, tumbling dice—the props of chance. It seemed somehow appropriate that they would pass through this gauntlet of probability on the way out, an apt reminder that, when it gets down to it, what they'd been talking about for four days was not so different in the end from what the poker players upstairs, awaiting their next card, were contemplating. Both get down to one word: risk.

Scholars consider risk one of the defining characteristics of the modern era, when man found he could play some role in predicting the future based on measurements of probability rooted in the patterns of the past. Peter L. Bernstein, an economist and institutional investor consultant, wrote an entire book on the subject, *Against the Gods: The Remarkable Story of Risk.* Mastering risk, Bernstein writes, is crucial to the "notion that the future is more than a whim of the gods and that men and women are not passive before nature."[27]

But who defines risk? How much risk is acceptable before action is taken? If so, whom do we aim to protect? Those are the essential questions of chemical regulation, and are as present in the debates over POPS as they are in every other controversy over chemicals. There is a corollary, too, on those gaming tables: What are my chances? Should I bet? Or fold? The answer is never perfectly clear; it is a play with uncertainty.

I would discover some months later that I wasn't the only one who saw that regulating chemicals is akin to a casino's games of chance. The EPA sees it that way too. One of the agency's key computerized tools for simulating the risks posed by chemicals is software with the apt name of "Monte Carlo." The program is, according to a promotional brochure, "named for Monte Carlo, Monaco, where the primary attractions are casinos containing games of chance. . . . The random behavior in games of chance is similar to how Monte Carlo simulation selects variable values at random to simulate a model." Two Polish mathematicians who were also card players, and wanted to see how close they could come to predicting their chances for a good hand, invented the program. The same principles, it seems, can be applied to chemical regulation.

One rainy afternoon I sat for two hours with Professor Thomas McKone, a professor of environmental health sciences at the University of California–Berkeley's Center for Environmental and Occupational Health. McKone's research on how chemicals behave in the environment is supported by National Science Foundation and EPA grants; he also works periodically as a consultant to the EU's Environment Directorate on risk assessments. I asked him to explain the basic difference between the European and American approach to limiting risks from exposure to chemicals. McKone flipped on his computer and invited me to join him in a Monte Carlo simulation. He has the program on his hard drive. The screen filled with a template of lines and columns in shades of black and white. The graphs were inexplicable to a layman like myself, but filled with meaning to a statistically minded scientist like McKone. "If it had been invented by Americans," he laughed, "'Monte Carlo' would have been called 'Las Vegas.'"[28]

McKone invented a chemical—which he named PBLX (and whose "invented" characteristics bore an uncanny resemblance to mercury). We were to assess the potential to poison people who eat fish who eat PBLX. "You run down the permutations like the values in a deck of cards," he said. McKone began inputting variables for his imaginary chemical, each with a numeric value dropped into a column: numbers of fish; concentration of PBLX in the water; concentration of the substance in each fish; how much fish from that area a person may be expected to eat; the solubility of PBLX; its potential to evaporate; how far it might travel. The lineup of variables seemed potentially endless. A curve rose on an accompanying graph with each changed input.

Finally, he stopped, pointed his figure at the uppermost level of the graph and said: "That's where you go if you want to protect the most people." He moved his finger down about half an inch: "And that's where you go if you want to protect less people, and on down. You get the picture?"

McKone, thankfully, explained: "The United States looks at the results on Monte Carlo and asks: 'Whom do we want to protect?' The Europeans, who do not use Monte Carlo, look at the properties of the chemical and say, 'How do we protect people from this chemical?' That is the basic difference."

The process, he said, can be manipulated. "You can skew that line down or up depending on the variables. That's why it's been pushed by industry: because the more complicated it gets, the more variables you put in, they come out ahead." That is, the more variables the EPA puts into Monte Carlo—genetics, behavior, alleged flaws in the scientific methods used to assess toxicity, benefits vs. costs—the less predictable the outcome, the less clear the danger. The outcome can be skewed like putting a marked card into a deck.

The result, in the United States, has been regulatory paralysis. But just as U.S. resistance led to a diplomatic blowback on the POPS treaty, similar effects can be seen now in the world's response to one of the country's most valued exports and tools of foreign policy, food—which is now being eyed with widespread suspicion as a result of the U.S. commitment to a technological fix that much of the world is rejecting.

5

Genetic Boomerang

Summers in the central mountain range of France, the Massif Centrale, are rich with the colors of wildflowers, the sound of tumbling waters, and the aromas of fruits and vegetables that have been cultivated here for hundreds of years. Country roads curl around idyllic small towns and the farms that surround them. Apples, plums, and pears hang heavy on the trees, and the yellow tassels of corn sway in the breezes for miles in every direction. It is beautiful and calm and long considered the bounteous soul—as the Midwest is to America—of France.

But the pastoral rhythms of this region, in the province of Auvergne, have been shaken by a conflict that strikes at the heart of the differences between America and Europe concerning one of those most primal of resources: food. One late night in August, 2005, those tensions came into high relief as forty-nine farmers assembled around a cornfield outside the town of Le Broc. The corn in Le Broc was close to four feet tall, about a month before it would be ready for harvest. It looked just like any other corn in the area, except that inside of each plant were genetically engineered genes created by the

FIVE

Monsanto Corporation. They had traveled a long way from Monsanto's laboratories in St. Louis, Missouri, where genes extracted from a bacterium were inserted into the corn's DNA to make a poison to kill one of the crop's most noxious pests, the corn borer.

The farmers marched onto the field and set to work. By three in the morning, they had torn more than two hundred plants from the earth. Cobs were scattered like trash along the side of the road, putting an ignoble end to one more season's experiment. Monsanto had hired a local farmer to grow the Le Broc test plot in hopes of gaining approval for commercial cultivation in France, the first step toward gaining the big-ticket goal of approval for all of Europe. For Monsanto, it has been a tumultuous road.

Three years earlier, in meetings across the French countryside, a grassroots farmers' movement had taken form, expressing alarm at what farmers felt was the potential for genetically modified crops, to alter the landscape that they and their predecessors had nurtured over centuries. Their manifesto expressed a willingness to take extreme measures to remove genetically modified organisms (GMOs) from the land. All participants agreed to the principles of nonviolence, and to the risks that could ensue. In the spirit of France's long history of "direct action," the farmers named themselves the Collectif des Faucheurs Volontaires (CFV), or Collective of Voluntary Reapers.

The most celebrated expression of this discontent had been the antiglobalization campaigner José Bové's attack on a McDonald's in 1999 in Millau, 120 miles to the southwest of Le Broc. The fast-food chain served as a convenient and irritating symbol of how globalization was changing the treasured values of French cuisine. Now one of the farmers' major concerns was how new genetically engineered plants, incorporating genes from other species, might breed with their own crops and undermine the biological purity of their corn and the quality and nutrition of their food. The farmers' movement was going beyond assaults on la cuisine americaine into defending the soil of la terre française.

By that night in Auvergne on August 1, more than five thousand farmers across the country had signed on as members of the collective, each one committed to engaging in what they call "preventive harvests"—stopping genetically engineered crops from coming to their natural fruition before they could be studied. Half of the GMO fields in France were destroyed by similar actions in 2005. Hundreds had been arrested and sentenced to prison terms and fines.

Two days later, the forty-nine preventive harvesters were arrested by local police. The arrests were not unanticipated; members of the group did little to hide their identity. All were charged at a regional court in the city of Orléans with criminal trespassing and the destruction of private property. State prosecutors asked for three-month jail terms for each of the participants in the Le Broc action, and Monsanto asked for damages of 398,000—about $450,000—to compensate the company for damages. For prosecutors, it was a simple case; the farmers didn't deny that they'd uprooted the corn.

The verdict, however, surprised the nation and sent a wake-up call across the Atlantic. All of the defendants were acquitted on grounds of self-defense. On behalf of the judicial tribunal in the city of Orléans, Judge Philippe Ouval-Molinos declared that "The defendants have shown proof that they committed an infraction of voluntary vandalism in . . . response to a situation of necessity." That "situation," the judge wrote, "resulted from the unbridled distribution of modified genes that constitutes a clear and present danger for the well-being of others, in the sense that it could be the source of contamination and unwanted pollution."[1] The court agreed with the defendants' assertion that their action was one of civil disobedience in defense of an agricultural system they argued was under siege by the spread of genetically engineered crops into France.

That verdict was later overturned on appeal (in France, plaintiffs as well as defendants are entitled to an appeal). The farmers were required to pay a 1,000 fine—approximately $1350.00—and one of them was sentenced to two months in jail. But the appeal did not slow the rising French resistance to GMOs, expressed with virulence in the fields, or through the cold shoulder of the market. Shortly afterward, another troop of voluntary harvesters broke into a Monsanto factory in southwest France, where they sought out GMO samples to "render them unusable." Dozens of attacks on GMO test plots marked the harvest season of 2006.[2] And though the French and European public generally is divided on those aggressive tactics, they are not divided on the targets of the farmers' ire: two-thirds to three-quarters of European consumers have consistently shown in public opinion polls an unwillingness to purchase any food products made with genetically engineered ingredients. The French farmers are afraid not only that their seed lines might be "contaminated" by new genetic material, but that if it happens their markets will collapse.

I contacted Monsanto's public relations officer, Christopher Horner, to ask about the company's response to the events in France, and he told me that there was no one in the company's St. Louis headquarters who "is familiar enough with what happened." He said he would inquire with his European colleagues, but over the course of ten months of inquiries did not provide any company official to be interviewed on this or any other genetic-engineering-related topic.[3]

What the French farmers fear, however, is precisely what has already happened in America's Corn Belt: the intrusion of genetically engineered genes into their corn. America's own corn farmers have discovered that their fate, their ability to continue with a profession that for many has been in the family for generations, could ride as much on the actions of their French counterparts and concerns of European consumers as the muscle and care they put into growing their own crops.[3]

Angoisse in the American Breadbasket

As the troop of CFV farmers were staging their nighttime raid on Monsanto's test plot, Laura Krause was sitting on the porch of her farmhouse in southeast Iowa, looking out disconsolately at her empty fields. Here in the heart of America's Corn Belt, on that Monday in August, it was another sweltering summer day. On this day, as on most days, Krause, in her broad-brimmed straw sun hat and overalls and lively blue eyes, looked like the icon of the American farmer. Indeed, in many ways she is: Krause runs an organic farm, just over a hundred acres of broccoli, potatoes, carrots, kale, and an "identity-preserved" corn seed, under the Abbe Hills label. That seed line had been developed by the first family of farmers to work her land, and she and previous owners of the land had sustained it for over a century. In a state that is one of America's breadbaskets — Iowa grows one fifth of the corn grown in the United States — Krause is one of four hundred and fifty organic farmers. Normally in August, her patch of cornfields would be fallow, crackling with insects and awaiting the planting that begins in September. But that September there would be no planting, nor had there been the September before. Krause's fields were laying involuntarily fallow because of a fateful trip she made to a grain elevator back in the spring of 2002.

In that year, a local laboratory informed Krause that her seed tested positive for the Bacillus thuringiensis (Bt) toxin, a similar genetic lineage to the one that Monsanto was trying to test for the French market in those fields in Le Broc. The Bt gene contains protein from a bacterium that prompts corn to produce a toxin that makes the corn borer's stomach explode. As an organic farmer, this was the last thing that Krause wanted in her corn.

I visited Krause on her farm shortly after she'd lost her organic certification.[4] Krause was devastated. Where traditional farmers apply pesticides, she counts on natural predators and aromatic repellents to keep the pests away; where traditional farmers apply herbicides to rid their fields of weeds, Krause and a crew do the weeding. It is a lot of work—all of which, suddenly, meant nothing in the cool calculus of the marketplace. From no fault of her own, the premium price she was accustomed to receiving for her organic seeds dropped from $3.50 a bushel to $1.75. No one compensated Krause for her losses.

I asked Krause where the genetically engineered ingredients she discovered in her seed could have come from. She took off her sun hat and raised it in her hand toward her neighbor's fields, spreading for miles into the horizon with the sunny yellow tassels of corn in its prime. "I'm surrounded by an ocean of genetically engineered corn," she said. Corn is a cross-pollinated crop; seeds can fly from the tassels, borne by the wind.[5] The genes could have come from any of her neighbors, or from a traveling bird, or from detritus left behind in the back of a delivery truck. She doesn't know. "It could have come from anywhere," Krause said, squinting into the sun.

Wherever the new unwanted ingredients came from, they destroyed her corn seed business. Her seed customers fled to other organic suppliers. When I spoke with her again three years later, she told me that she had been trying, slowly, to reconstitute her organic crop by letting the ground lay fallow, in other words, not planting anything. Krause told me she was attempting to breed out those genes left behind in the soil, with the aide of "new gene stock from Uruguay and Argentina" supplied to her by the botany department at Iowa State University. She was hoping to regain the organic integrity of her identity-preserved seed crop and lure back her customers.[6]

It turns out that Laura Krause is not alone. The Union of Concerned Scientists tested American seed corn in 2004 and detected the presence of at least some levels of genetically engineered material in 50 percent of the samples.[7] The French did not have to look far to find other examples of GMO contamination. In Spain, the only country in Europe with large-scale commercial growing of GMO crops (and limited to use as cattle feed), Greenpeace reported that 25 percent of non-genetically-engineered corn samples in the rich agricultural regions of Aragon and Catalonia had traces of GMOs; numerous growers lost their certification and the price for their crop dropped by one third.[8] The GMO Contamination Register, a website that tracks incidences as they occur, lists dozens of contamination events between 2004 and 2006 in twenty-five countries; contaminated crops include corn, rice, soybeans, papaya, rapeseed, and canola.[9]

Contamination may seem like an abstract issue to most Americans, who are not farmers and who have generally exhibited far less wariness toward genetically modified crops than their European counterparts. One third of America's corn is neither organic nor genetically engineered, but traditionally hybridized corn. Laura Krause, like other American farmers who choose not to grow genetically modified corn, are now paying the price for the unwanted consequences of a technology they did not ask for. They are discovering that their economic fate is tied, through the complex connections of the agricultural commodities market, to the efforts of those French farmers to remove Monsanto's fingerprints from their soil, and from the sentiments of European consumers who don't want them in their supermarkets.

Who's Not Coming to Dinner

When widespread cultivation of GMOs was still a dream in a laboratory, then vice president Dan Quayle declared the federal government's position about these new organisms that contained genes never before seen in a plant. Genetically engineered crops were, he stated in 1992, the "significant equivalent" of other types of traditionally grown crops. That fundamental principle provides the foundation for the U.S. government's position; GMOs have faced few restrictions on cultivation ever since. The United States Department of Agriculture poured $250 million into helping develop, and then promote, agricultural biotechnology, which exploded across American farm country. Less than 1 percent of that total, $1.6 million, was put into assessing the risks. Since the first genetically engineered corn seed was introduced into commercial production in 1996, 61 percent of U.S. cornfields are now planted with varieties manipulated in one way or another with the genes of species other than plants. Eighty-nine percent of soybeans have been genetically engineered, most of them with Monsanto's Roundup Ready modified gene, rendering them resistant to Monsanto's own herbicide Roundup.[10] Increasing percentages of wheat, canola, and other crops are being grown with genetically engineered ingredients. Indeed, genetically engineered ingredients are everywhere in U.S. supermarkets—in processed corn syrup, in soft drinks, cereals, canned vegetables, candy. They are now an omnipresent, though hidden, presence in America's food.

Genetically modified organisms also clearly offer a real allure to many American farmers: from resistance to pests, frost, heat, drought, and other factors that can devastate whole fields in a season, the new seeds were being bred to reduce the risks from making a livelihood off the land. Some environmentalists had even promoted genetic engineering as a means of decreasing the applications of toxic pesticides and relying on genetically engineered pest resistance instead. Proponents faced a challenge, however: how do you prove a negative, that genetically engineered crops are not unsafe? In the United States, Vice President Quayle's declaration had provided an important government imprimatur: the new food crops were essentially the same as naturally evolved varieties, so no special attention to their ecological or health consequences was warranted. Europeans, however, were skeptical of a new technology that had barely been tested before being unleashed wholesale into the American food system.

So few studies had been done about the safety of genetically engineered crops that while no one could prove they did actual harm, no one could prove the opposite either, that they were benign. Europe was coming out of a tailspin provoked by the raging controversy over mad cow disease, which spread into European stockyards despite assurances from public officials and scientists that there was nothing to worry about. If the idea that cows were getting sick from eating the ground-up remains of their fellow heifers was not sci-fi enough, here was another development straight out of surrealism: corn or strawberries being bred with the genes of fish or pigs. A popular movement erupted in Europe against the introduction of genetic engineering into food.

The battle over Europe's GMO policy was really the first great transatlantic environmental fight. That policy was sketched out in the European Parliament, which devised a strategy for halting the spread of the new technology until its effects on the environment and human health could be more thoroughly understood. In 1998, a temporary moratorium was declared on the imports of any food or seeds containing genetically modified ingredients, so scientists could pursue further study.

Some of those studies, conducted at scientific institutions in Europe and the United States, would show cause for concern: differences in physiological structure from traditionally bred crops; the run-off of toxins inbred into the plants themselves were affecting other crops; and signs in some experimental varieties of disruptive effects on the kidney and other organs of test animals who consumed them. A primary concern was also the potential for intermixing of genetically engineered with non-genetically engineered crops, creating new DNA combinations that those French farmers back in Le Broc were attempting to avoid, and which Laura Krause had already discovered back in Iowa.[11]

Karin Scheele is the Austrian member of the European Parliment who shepherded the EU's policy on GMOs through the parliament. Central casting could not have invented a more perfect counterpart to Laura Krause in her fields. The two women actually resemble one another. Scheele dresses in down-to-earth pantsuits, her curly blond hair framing a broad face and mischievous blue eyes. She is the daughter of farmers and represents the district of Upper Austria, that country's agricultural mother lode, with abundant corn, dairy, and apple farms.

We were sitting in Scheele's office on the tenth floor of the Parliament as she recalled the intensive lobbying by U.S. industry and the State Department as they tried to reopen Europe's markets to American genetically engineered food exports. She was at the time the Socialist Party's ranking member on the Environment Committee, and one of the lead figures developing a policy that would replace the temporary moratorium with an approval process for GMOs based on scientific review, as well as guidelines for labeling GMO products after their approval.

For the Bush administration and the biotech industry, Scheele was key to reopening Europe's lucrative market. The Clinton administration had also been an avid proponent of exporting America's agricultural biotechnology, and was equally unsuccessful in convincing the Europeans to ease their strict controls. European farmers had the potential to make the difference for firms like Monsanto, DuPont, Pioneer, and others making a profit or turning a loss on their multibillion-dollar investments in genetic engineering. Into her office, she recalled, came representatives from the U.S. State and Commerce departments, from the American Chamber of Commerce, from Monsanto, DuPont, Syngenta, and Dow, the major producers of genetically engineered seed, three out of four of which are U.S. firms (Syngenta is Swiss). Suddenly, a previously unknown Austrian (to Americans anyway) was being courted by some of the most powerful diplomats and corporate officials in the world.

Scheele told me she was surprised at the abundant attention suddenly being paid to her from the other side of the Atlantic. But the U.S. embrace had little effect. "From my point of view," she recalled, "someone coming here from the Chamber of Commerce, I know they are paid to represent U.S. industry. I'm not paid to do that. I was clear to them: I'm representing the interests of European citizens."[12]

Scheele vividly recalled a meeting which highlighted the diametrically different approaches between the United States and Europe on GMOs. She remembers the date precisely; it was March 23, 2003, she says, because it was three days after the launch of the U.S. invasion of Iraq (an event not fondly remembered in the chambers of the Parliament).

Scheele's light-filled office features a spectacular view of downtown Brussels, but it is not spacious; it can fit about five comfortably. She had to obtain extra chairs from colleagues down the hall to accommodate a U.S. delegation, including representatives from the State Department, Commerce Department, and U.S. Trade, who trooped into her office that day. She was there with her legislative assistant, Sigrid Semlitsch.

"It was just me and Sigrid and about ten American men gathered around my little desk here," she recalled. A State Department official opened the discussion in a friendly tone: "He said, 'We're not talking about convincing intellectuals like you. We need to talk about using GMOs together to fight poverty and hunger.'" Scheele laughs at the recollection: "I never thought of myself as an intellectual before that moment! I come from an agricultural district in north Austria. I didn't read Karl Marx. I wasn't sure whether he was insulting intellectuals by calling me one, or trying to flatter me with something I never thought I was. . . . I was thinking, 'Stop this bullshit!'"

Scheele didn't say that of course, but she did respond with its diplomatic equivalent: "You want to fight poverty? Why is your administration cutting foreign aid? Why is your administration taking South Africa to the WTO on low-cost pharmaceuticals? Why are you cutting back in money for family planning?"

The meeting did not end happily. As they departed, the U.S. delegates' final message was clear, Scheele recalls: "You won't survive the WTO." Two months later, the United States, along with Canada and Argentina, pulled that trump card and filed a World Trade Organization complaint against the European Union's GMO moratorium—asserting it constituted a "barrier to trade" and was costing international producers hundreds of millions of dollars in lost sales.

The World Trade Organization case was argued in Geneva through 2005. In September 2006, the WTO issued its decision: the EU's moratorium on GMO imports amounted to a blanket ban on products from other countries; it was an illegal barrier to trade.[13] The WTO's decision found that the Europeans could block the import of an entire class of products without risk assessment of individual varieties. But by the time the case was decided against Europe, the ban that the WTO ruled against was no longer in place. The EU had already lifted the moratorium and replaced it with a case-by-case assessment process, putting genetically engineered organisms through scientific review. The system that Scheele and many others had labored on for five years was in place. Scheele herself would have preferred an outright ban—which her native Austria would soon try, unsuccessfully, to impose on its own—but the system was far more rigorous in its review of GMOs' potential downsides than any now reigning in the United States.[14]

The EU case-by-case approval process for GMOs requires the submission of environmental and health data to the European Food Safety Agency (EFSA) for review prior to approval for commercial cultivation. It was to this agency where, several generations later, that corn in Le Broc would have been destined to travel had those plants grown to maturity. Thus far, seventeen varieties have been approved for cultivation in Europe; in the United States, the number of genetically engineered varieties under cultivation numbers in the hundreds and is growing. All European varieties are subject to "coexistence" requirements—buffer zones distancing genetically engineered fields from non-genetically engineered fields, to prevent cross-pollination.

The EU added caveats to its new regulations, reflecting the high levels of uncertainty that remain about the long-term environmental and health impacts of GMOs. For starters, all GMO-containing products must be labeled. Those labels turn out to be the equivalent of a skull and crossbones, given the high level of resistance among European consumers to GMOs. Major retail outlets across Europe have declared they will sell no genetically engineered produce or processed goods, including supermarket chains in Great Britain, Germany, the Netherlands, Belgium, and France.[15] Almost all GMOs grown in Europe now are destined for cattle feed.

Labeling has proved controversial in the United States: the industry has spent hundreds of thousands of dollars to oppose, thus far successfully, state and county level legislative and initiative campaigns in California, Missouri, Oregon, Washington, Rhode Island, and elsewhere that would require labeling of genetically engineered ingredients in food.

Scheele recalled with still-simmering indignation the pressure the agricultural biotech industry and their administration allies put on European legislators, for what seemed to her to be a simple matter of informing consumers about what is contained in the food they eat. "The Americans," she said, "are always pushing for a market economy, for market reforms. But when the market decides against their own products, they like to push the market away."

"In the United States," Scheele continued, "if something is not proven dangerous, then put it on the market and don't bother people with the details, with the choices. In Europe, there is more consciousness about problematic questions around GMOs, potential environmental disadvantages. The consumer has a right to know what these are, and what he or she is buying."

Another significant caveat by the Europeans was contained in an Environmental Liability Directive—which affirms the basic principle that those who cause environmental damage are obligated to pay to remediate that damage.[16] For GMOs, this means that manufacturers can be held liable for future damages yet unseen from farmers' use of their high-technology seeds. Member states are required to include provisions in their national laws offering compensation, with funds generated by a "GMO tax," to farmers whose crops are "contaminated" by gene flow from GMOs. Denmark has already implemented such a tax; other countries are in the process of devising schemes to ensure such protections. The European Union also requires what it calls "traceability"—each shipment of GMO food must have a clear paper trail, so if contamination or some other problem occurs, the source of it is clear. Member states may also require that distance be maintained between GMO-approved fields and non-GMOs.

Had Laura Krause been farming in Denmark, for example, and not Iowa, the closest GMO field could not have been next door, but no less than two hundred meters, one fifth of a mile away. Had her fields been contaminated, she would have received compensation to make up for the 50 percent drop in price that occurred after discovering the unwanted genetic material in her corn. She also would have been able to identify the source of that contamination because of the "traceability" requirement.

The EU's qualified acceptance of GMOs has created unease even within Europe. Member states have attempted to defy the European Commission's demand to keep their markets open to GMOs, just as American states have historically attempted to assert their authority over that of the federal government. In December 2006, nineteen of the EU's twenty-five members voted against the commission's request that Austria lift its ban on two genetically engineered corn varieties, one of which is made by Monsanto, that had been approved for use in Europe. Both Hungary and Poland have refused to approve the cultivation of seventeen different Monsanto lines of genetically modified corn seeds. Across Europe, 166 regional governments have instituted safety provisions so strict that these regions—from small rural districts in Italy and Poland to an entire province in Austria—are, in effect, GMO free.

At the same time, regions are striking independent trade deals as a means of ensuring that no GMO products enter their territory. The French province of Brittany, for example, has an ongoing import agreement with the Brazilian state of Manas Gerais to supply GMO-free corn and soybeans, a deal that was specifically driven by the province's desire for non-GMO grain.[17] Fifteen years ago that deal for corn and soybeans could very well have been struck with the state of Iowa or any other corn-producing American state, which long was a major supplier of grains to Europe. Despairing of there ever being a significant market for GMOs inside Europe, the Swiss company Syngenta pulled its entire GMO division out of Europe and relocated it to the United States. (In 2005, Swiss citizens, who are not members of the EU, but who do provide a home to the World Trade Organization, voted to ban all GMOs from cultivation in Switzerland for ten years.) The EU's ongoing reluctance to accept the unchecked import of GMOs continues to tarnish U.S.–EU relations: in May 2007, Friends of the Earth-Europe unearthed documents from the U.S. trade representative asking the European Commission to loosen its scientific review process and limit the abilities of nations and regions to impose more strict standards of GMOs than Brussels.[18]

The most poignant effects of the imploding market for America's genetically altered food exports are felt among the 30 percent of

American corn farmers, and higher percentages of farmers growing rice, wheat, and other essential commodities, who do not use genetically engineered technology but who are caught in the spiraling decline of desirability for what was once a source of profit and livelihood. Food was once a potent weapon of U.S. diplomacy, but holds little leverage today among countries that reject the technology that lies behind it. A treasured image that Americans have of themselves—"breadbasket to the world"—is being rejected by overseas consumers who once accepted American food gratefully and without question.

Much of the world has followed Europe's lead. In addition to the European Union, more than thirty countries, including Japan (which has even tougher standards than Europe), have imposed tight restrictions on the import of GMO crops. When a food crisis swept southern Africa, two of the countries hardest hit—Zambia and Zimbabwe—refused the U.S. offer of corn and soybean donations out of fear they would introduce genetically engineered material into their own agriculture (and thus, also, eliminate them forever from contention as future exporters to Europe). In 2005, the African Union expressed resistance to a U.S. aid program that encourages the planting of GMOs, indicating its preference for a German aid program that encourages non-GMO cultivation. Many of those who were once avid consumers of American food exports do not want what American farmers are producing.

The Blowback

The effect of this rejection has been disastrous in American farm country. The U.S. Department of Agriculture's Economic Research Service reports that in 1996, prior to the widespread introduction of GMOs, the United States exported 3.15 million metric tons of corn to the then-fifteen member states of the European Union. That accounted for 82 percent of European corn imports. By 1997, that figure was starting to drop rapidly; by 2003, it had plunged to 37,000 metric tons and by 2005 had dropped to 33,000 metric tons—barely enough corn to fill a single shipload. Over ten years, tracking almost perfectly the span in which genetically engineered food became a dominant force in the U.S. food system, there has been a 90 percent collapse of what was once one of America's strongest export markets.[19]

Dan McGuire, Policy Chairman of the American Corn Growers Association, owns a corn farm in his native Nebraska and has watched the destruction of various U.S. agricultural export markets from the inside. He remembers well the days a decade ago and earlier, when large quantities of U.S. corn were shipped down to New Orleans and other U.S. ports and onto freighters for export to the European Union.

As markets around the world dry up, grain elevators across the Corn Belt have been overflowing with unsold grain. The other end of America's declining corn export markets have been the rapid rise in corn inventories: According to the Economic Resource Service, the rise in what it calls "corn ending stocks," (i.e., the amount of corn left in storage silos rather than sold) also tracks the rise in the spread of GMOs: in the nine years following 1996, corn inventories rose steadily to a record breaking 2.4 billion bushels in 2005.[20] And while the amount of unsold corn rises, prices head in the opposite direction. "That inventory," McGuire told me, "knocks hell out of the price of corn."[21] The ACGA calculates that the shrinking demand for U.S. exports has led to a drop in corn prices of at least $1.20 per bushel over the past five years as a result of increased inventory. They estimate that the refusal of foreign buyers to accept any type of U.S. corn because of fears it may contain genetically engineered varieties is costing farmers at least two hundred million dollars a year in lower prices due to lost sales. Big grain producers like China, Brazil, and the Ukraine are entering the breech, and taking America's place by supplying non-genetically engineered corn and other crops to Europe and the many other countries that are following its lead. Meanwhile, the Economic Research Service reports that the use of genetically engineered seeds, which come with a higher price tag for the farmer than traditionally bred seeds—and a lower cost for inputs like pesticides and herbicides—has still not meant an overall improvement in the financial status of American farmers.

In Iowa farm country, one of the more tragic effects of America's isolation on genetically engineered food has been a boom time for auctioneers. Bankrupted farmers are selling their land and their homes while the bottom drops out of their foreign markets. Ironically, for those farmers who remain the rising gap between their income and their costs is compensated by subsidies from the federal government. As prices drop, subsidies provided by the Commodity Credit Corporation to farmers increase to compensate for loss of income. Thus, the thirty-five billion dollars in payments to corn farmers during that span of plummeting prices from 1996 to 2005 amounted, at least partially, to a personal subsidy by every American taxpayer to the agricultural biotechnology industry. These are the very same subsidies that were at the heart of disputes during the Doha round of trade meetings in 2006. The only thing saving corn farmers today from further economic crisis is the new market for ethanol, which has reduced corn inventories and raised prices in 2006 and 2007.

The French-American Connection

The attack of the preventive harvesters in Le Broc prompted an unprecedented response by the police in the French province of Auvergne. Huge spotlights were installed around the GMO test fields to illuminate them at night. "They've got policemen with guns and dogs walking around those fields now," recalled Arnaud Apoteken, head of the anti-GMO campaign for Greenpeace France shortly after the arrests of the CFV farmers. "The countryside that normally inspires feelings of tranquility now feels like a war zone."[22] In the fertile lands of Auvergne, the police patrol cornfields packed with genes created by a company in America's farm country that is repelling consumers around the world from American food.

A hundred miles north of the St. Louis birthplace of those seeds, the Illinois River flows past the historic city of Springfield, Illinois. The scene along the riverfront is classic Americana, saturated with the aromas of grain and abuzz with the engines of open-air trailers piled high with the bounty of Midwest agriculture. Had the customers of Laura Krause the opportunity to export corn grown with her seed, they would have sent it from Springfield. Barges line up along the docks to load up with corn, soybeans, and other crops supplied by the farmers of Iowa and the upper Midwest, for the trip south along the Illinois to the Mississippi River and the Gulf of Mexico. In times past, the grain piled high in those barges would be sent to Europe and beyond. Here you don't see policemen, but what you do see is a sight new in our era, the American mirror image of those French police. At every grain elevator along these docks are men and women whose job it is to screen out the ingredients that have caused such concern among the farmers of Auvergne and among the consumers of Europe. Their job is to test crops for signs of genetic engineering.

Larry Keene, a representative of Growmark, a grain processing cooperative that sends grain down the Illinois, explained to me that any farmer who hopes to load his corn onto a ship headed downriver for export must first have it tested at the grain elevator.[23] The testing has become an unavoidable step at the transit depots of U.S. agriculture. Testers of GMOs are the flip side of the auctioneers; the presence of the former has contributed to the rise of the latter. Farmers are accustomed to dealing with the vagaries of the weather, of moisture levels, of pests and unforeseen diseases. Here on the docks, however, on the verge of determining what their previous seasons of labor has been worth, farmers now have one new variable with which to contend. An entirely new product line has been created by the biotech firm Strategic Diagnostics, Inc. to ensure that U.S. crops do not go where they are not wanted.

I spoke with Mark Kimbale, international accounts manager at Strategic Diagnostics, Inc. headquarters in Delaware, who explained that the procedure is much like a pregnancy test, with a twist.[24] Each truck that pulls into a grain elevator waits before unloading, while a huge automated snout sucks up grain from different parts of the truck. The three or four samples from each load are suctioned back to a lab in the elevator, where they're combined, ground, and mixed with water. A technician drops a Strategic Diagnostics-designed dipstick—it's called a lateral flow strip—into the sample. "In five minutes," Kimbale said, "it tells you right there whether it's positive or negative." Instead of pregnancy (or not), a red stripe signifies the presence of at least one engineered gene, and a red and a blue stripe tells the farmer that there are multiple foreign genes in his corn. These are known in the trade as "singular or multiple 'genetic events.'" And having one or another of those is known as "bad news."

I asked Kimbale what happens if there is a positive result. Kimbale, who's on the technical side of the operation, didn't know: "We don't hear about the results," he said. "We're just focused on creating as accurate a test as possible."

But Larry Keene, who monitors that river traffic as part of his job at Growmark, knew the answer. "That colored stripe," Keene said, "means the load is rejected as 'identity preserved,' and the farmer is then free to do with it as he likes." The farmer faces a simple choice: sell his crop on the spot for a price that drops anywhere from ten to fifty cents a bushel, or bring it home, where it can rot within a week.

The farmers of Le Broc and the farmers of Iowa, it seems, are on a single möbius strip, the gears in their reapers are riding on the same belt, buffeted by interests on either side of the Atlantic that are way beyond their control. Hacking away at those Monsanto cornstalks, France's "voluntary reapers" had stumbled unwittingly onto an essential link between their rising fury at what they fear, and the fate that is already befalling American farmers.

The phenomenon is not limited to corn. Other genetically engineered crops in the United States include canola, rapeseed, tomatoes, and lettuce. In the fall of 2006, Strategic Diagnostics, Inc. heard some more good news for the company: they'd be gaining a new set of farmers interested in their testing technology. Shipments of American rice found to be contaminated with an experimental variety of a genetically engineered rice called Liberty Link had been sent to Europe and Japan, where they were not authorized for sale or consumption. Further shipments of all American long-grain rice were stopped by the national authorities. Genetically engineered rice is not yet in widespread cultivation in the United States; the contaminant was an experimental variety made by Bayer Crop Sciences. "We got a panicked call from some of our growers," Kimbale recalled, "who wanted a test for rice." The company made a new lateral test strip targeting genetically engineered ingredients in rice within a week; it is now in use across the rice-growing areas of America. A class-action lawsuit was filed on behalf of three hundred farmers in Arkansas, Missouri, Mississippi, Louisiana, Texas, and California asking for damages from Bayer. The price for American rice dropped by 10 percent after the contamination was discovered and continued dropping through the end of the year.[25]

Whether one thinks GMOs are harmful or not—the evidence is not clear on either side—the price is being paid now, by American farmers, for the unwillingness of the United States to entertain questions about a technology to which it committed at least a quarter of a billion dollars in public funds to develop (research that has benefited primarily the companies that are now profiting from the seeds). We will see what happens in very different circumstances when the questions that the American government has not asked, about how some of the country's major industries construct their products, leaves them playing catch-up to Europe. From that conflict, though, there may be some surprise beneficiaries: Americans.

Rise and Fall of the Machine

In the southwest of Brussels, a three-hundred-foot-tall molecule rises along the edge of the Laeken Park. The molecule, made of steel and glass and magnified 165 billion times, has been there since the world's fair of 1958. In that year, as a gesture to the exciting new technologies developed after World War II, Belgium commissioned the molecule as its host pavilion. They called it the Atomium.

It was the 1950s, and the Atomium was intended to be a symbolic celebration of all the marvels of technology—which, when you get down to it, really is the business of manipulating molecules. In the words of an exhibition catalog, the Atomium "symbolized a democratic desire for peace between nations, faith in technical progress (despite fears about the atom bomb) and optimism about the future of a modern world that promised to enhance people's lives."

As the years passed, the Atomium became an icon of Brussels itself; inside there have been forty-plus years of exhibits featuring artists and designers both celebrating and commenting on technology. It was one of the first modern institutions to mix technology with art, and helped to elevate the reputation of so-called kinetic art, the art of moving parts. As the world changed, so did the exhibits, which began reflecting the darkening luster with which we have come to approach technological innovation. A sense of dark humor and irony, qualities for which Belgians are justifiably renowned, began to be reflected in the exhibits as the world came to understand that there might be a price to be paid for all that infectious cheerleading of technological progress.

Among the many artists whose works have been featured at the Atomium is one of my favorites, the Swiss sculptor Jean Tinguely, a pioneer of kinetic art well known for his giant mechanical creations. Tinguely once famously stated: "In life, the only stable thing is movement, always and everywhere," and his work has always reflected this exaltation of kinetic energy. Tinguely made enormous machines of whirring wheels and gears, whose intricate hinges and flapping parts have a kind of beautiful balance and even musical rhythm. They evoke a kind of grinding perfection, in which the moving parts cling, clang, and roll off and over one another—until they, and this has been a Tinguely trademark, self-destruct. Tinguely's self-destroying machines are epic in their size and intricacy, and their temporary home at the Atomium, monument to technology, seemed apt, for they are like a sped-up look at what is built into the insides of every mechanical device: its own death.

In trying to imagine what happens to the millions of parts and thousands of chemical ingredients that age, decay, and slowly implode, I try to think of a Tinguely machine—miniature versions of which are in everything from iPods to DVD players, from toasters to the computer on which these words are being written. Sometimes the parts are large, like in an automobile, and sometimes infinitesimally small, like in a cell phone. But no matter their size, the one thing they have in common is they die. And then what happens?

Machine Mortality

Across the United States and Europe, there is growing recognition that the dynamic of construction and destruction embodied in those marvelous Tinguely machines is not a simple metaphor. Electronic waste is emerging as one of the central challenges of our era. Plug something into a wall or a battery and wonderful things can happen. But conjuring that action often requires the conductive, adhesive, and cohering qualities of some of the most toxic substances known — things like lead, mercury, and cadmium. Operating within the confined space of a well-sealed appliance or car engine, their mobility into the environment or your bloodstream is limited. But once their usable life span is finished, it's a different story.

The numbers are enormous. Three billion consumer electrical products will be scrapped worldwide by 2010, according to the International Association of Electronics Recyclers. More than one hundred million computers, monitors, and televisions become obsolete each year in the United States alone, according to the Environmental Protection Agency, "most of which" will end up sitting in basements or back rooms or backyards awaiting disposal, and slowly leach their chemically hazardous ingredients into the environment.[1] Every year, the United Nations Environment Program estimates that twenty to fifty million metric tons of e-waste are added to that heap.[2] Look around your home: follow the trail from the wires plugged into their sockets, count the toasters, televisions, microwave ovens, DVD players, light bulbs, and other electronic goods; add to that medical devices in hospitals and sophisticated electronic equipment in offices and factories; multiply by several hundred million, and you can do your own calculations as to the dimensions of that future mass of electrical detritus.

Like a self-destroying Jean Tinguely machine, this bounty of obsolescence ends up in a big pile of collapsed circuitry. The components decay, spring leaks, form cracks; their connections dissolve, and the atmospheric forces of moisture and heat work their destructive tricks. The minerals and chemicals that once held that shiny whatever-it-is together disperse into the environment. The EPA has concluded that e-waste is growing nearly three times faster than municipal waste.[3] They are the components of a time-release toxic debt-load for the multiplicity of cool and complicated electronic connections of modern life.

Resetting the Periodic Table

As I was writing this book, my printer, a five-year-old Epson 777 inkjet, died. Who knew the reason? Probably it was just age. I didn't bother to find out. My options at that stage were several: I could drop it in the trash can for pickup at my home and it would be ground up along with all my other household garbage; living in San Francisco, I could bring it to a city-sponsored recycling center, which would extract its still-functioning parts and turn it into a used printer for somebody else (one of the few such programs in the United States); or I could drop it off at a scrap yard, which means that it would most likely be sent elsewhere, off to some squalid dump in one of any number of developing countries hungry for the precious metals and parts. There, it would be worked over by people without the slightest protection from the multiple toxins contained inside. The latter turns out to be by far the most favored "recycling" or "disposal" option in the United States and, until recently, in Europe.

The Basel Action Network, a Seattle-based non-governmental organization, sent investigators around the world and determined that at least 50 percent of the used cell phones, computers, televisions, and other e-waste that is collected for recycling in the United States is shipped overseas to scrap yards in places like Taiwan, the

Philippines, Nigeria, and China, where oversight has been minimal, at best.[4] In Europe, Greenpeace International tracked European shipments of e-waste overseas, and found it in Chinese and Indian scrap yards, with dangerously high levels of lead, mercury, and cadmium in the dust that workers routinely inhale.[5] In some areas of China, where e-waste from both continents has been collected into huge open pits, river-water samples taken in 2005 contained levels of lead and other metals from ten to twenty-four thousand times what World Health Organization standards consider safe in drinking water.[6]

The Basel Action Network is named after a treaty, the Basel Convention, which was written in Basel, Switzerland in 1994, and which prohibits the export of hazardous wastes from developed countries to developing ones. The Convention designates e-waste as hazardous waste because of its toxic ingredients. As of 2006, 166 countries had ratified the convention—including the entire European Union as a body, and each of the member states individually. The United States is alone among developed countries in not ratifying it.[7]

Even Europe, however, was slow in implementing a serious approach to e-waste, as Greenpeace's findings reveal. But in 2003, the EU began trying to get a handle on electronic waste. They started with recycling: the Waste in Electrical and Electronic Equipment Directive mandated that by the end of 2006, 75 to 80 percent of the components in electrical equipment, by weight, be recyclable. The EU encouraged research into materials that were less toxic and would biodegrade over time. More than seventy products fall under the purview of the directive, including computers, washing machines, refrigerators, vacuum cleaners, toasters, medical devices, radiotherapy equipment, fluorescent lamps, television sets, video games, cordless telephones, candy vending machines, and "automatic dispensers for hot or cold bottles or cans."[8] Responsibility for handling the costs of recycling was placed with the manufacturers themselves, who were mandated to develop their own "take-back" programs, where they would be held accountable for the proper handling of the waste generated by their products at the end of their natural life cycle. Suddenly, hundreds of firms discovered that they had to come up with new materials inside their machines—which they, and not some distant dump in China or Nigeria, would have to process safely, recycling what they could. The result has been the creation of "take-back" stations in retail outlets across Europe—including office-supply stores selling Epsons—where e-waste is collected and processed in an environmentally sound manner.

Rosalinde van der Vlies, an administrator in the EU's Environment Directorate, explained to me that at the core of the EU's policy is a "life-cycle analysis" applied to all consumer products: an assessment of the actual costs over the lifetime of consumer products, from their creation to their demise.[9]

Traditionally, production "costs" center on a narrow set of fixed factors: labor, facilities maintenance, natural resources, and energy use, the literal costs of production. But van der Vlies and her colleagues have been attempting to ascertain the entirety of real costs involved—including those that have been borne by society as a whole, such as the costs of cleaning up toxic pollution or the health-care costs borne by the victims of chemical exposure for which producers historically have taken no responsibility. Suddenly, what looks cheap to the producer and individual consumer turns out to be expensive to society. The core of the Europeans' philosophical shift is the insistence that the producers must now share costs long borne by society at large—that is, taxpayers—as well.

To get a better understanding of how such costs are actually calculated, I spoke with Mike Wallace, who works for the U.S. office of a British consulting firm called TruCost. The company, headquartered in London, consults with businesses on a new set of mandates for reporting profit-loss statements for firms trading on the European stock exchanges.

In response to the corporate scandals that shook the financial worlds on both sides of the Atlantic—ENRON in the United States and the Italian firm Parmalat being among the more high-profile examples—both Europe and the United States passed new measures intended to ensure greater corporate financial accountability. In the United States, the bill known as Sarbanes-Oxley imposed far tighter requirements on corporations to ensure transparency and heighten the distance between corporate auditors and their employers. The Europeans followed suit with the Accounts Modernisation Directive, which has similar goals to Sarbanes-Oxley. But that directive adds several major components missing from Sarbanes-Oxley: most importantly, it requires publicly traded European firms to include future environmental liabilities in their accounting of costs and potential future profits. Companies must disclose, for example, future toxic-waste cleanup charges; penalties on inefficient energy consumption; liability for chemical poisonings among workers or consumers; or the potential for rising marketplace distaste for environmentally unappealing products.

For those who have ever attempted to decipher the meaning of all those numbers and graphs in corporate financial reports, the directive also thankfully adds a requirement that companies provide a narrative rendering of the political and regulatory atmosphere in which they are operating, and the potential environmental liabilities they may face in the future.

"What the Europeans are saying," Wallace explained, "is that costs that have been externalized will no longer be paid for by society."[10] Wallace said that until now the lack of reporting of such potential liabilities has had the effect of inflating the value of companies that may be forced to contend with the price of environmental irresponsibility, or that attempt to shift those costs onto the public. A profit-and-loss statement that does not include either current or future environmental liability paints a falsely rosy picture of a company's financial future. In this way, life-cycle analysis, while conjuring some vaguely Buddhist overtones, in fact has a hard-nosed economic rationale at its core.

In the United States, industry has consistently opposed imposition of end-of-life principles that they are busy implementing in Europe. Efforts to institute a nationwide recycling plan have been resisted by the electronics industry. In 2005 the EPA withdrew support from its own National Electronic Product Stewardship Initiative (NEPSI), which was intended to establish a financing system to facilitate a nationwide system for the recycling and reuse of used electronics. The electronics industry, the agency concluded, could not agree on a jointly coordinated approach. Instead, the EPA substituted a series of voluntary programs that the Government Accountability Office determined, in November 2005, were ineffective. American companies and recyclers, the GAO concluded in its assessment of large-scale recycling programs, prefer the "more convenient option of simply throwing these products away," and face no disincentives to simply shipping "used electronics . . . to overseas buyers with no guarantee that they will be properly handled."[11] In early 2007, the computer giant Dell indicated its willingness to test out a take-back program, signaling the first U.S. industry-driven effort to offer services in the United States already being offered in Europe.

States have begun moving into the vacuum left by the federal government's inaction. California, Maryland, Maine, and Washington have instituted their own "take-back" programs, assessing a fee on the manufacturers of computers to finance their eventual recycling. These were passed into law over industry objections. Barbara Kyle, coordinator for the Computer TakeBack Campaign in San Jose, in the heart of California's Silicon Valley, commented: "Industries will work with governments on [electronic] waste in one country in Europe and then turn their back and do something completely different in another. In Europe or Japan they'll concede that recycling helps improve product designs, but in the United States they'll say it has no positive effects on design. It's a real double standard."[12]

The EU's follow-up effort on e-waste confronted what's actually inside all those electronic devices to begin with. The restriction of hazardous substances directive, or RoHS, requires that manufacturers remove four toxic metals—lead, cadmium, chromium, and mercury—that have been critical ingredients in hundreds of thousands of products in everything from computers and semiconductors to electric trains and cell phones. It also bans the use of polybrominated flame retardants, the same ones proposed for the POPS list by Norway and the European Union. All these substances are considered by the EU as having potent carcinogenic or neurologically toxic effects.[13]

Electronics is one of the most global of industries. Soon it would be clear how far the U.S. government had fallen behind even the industry itself. American-made or designed electrical appliances and high-tech products travel the world. U.S. manufacturers exported $199 billion worth of electronic goods in 2005, just over $43 billion of which was to the European Union.[14] Other major electrical producers in Taiwan, Korea, China, and Japan export tens of billions of dollars of electrical goods to both the United States and to Europe. Of course European manufacturers—Phillips, Siemens, and others—are also major exporters to the United States. RoHS challenged a trillion-dollar industry that has penetrated into almost every household in America and Europe.

I caught up with Michael Kirschner, the consultant we met in chapter 1 during his session on RoHS in Silicon Valley, at his office in downtown San Francisco, just a month before RoHS took effect on July 1, 2006. He had been traveling the country explaining RoHS to anxious engineers in Chicago, Houston, Boston, and Detroit. His office is located in an alleyway in the center of San Francisco's South of Market district, home to many of the high-tech innovations that have spread around the world over the past decade. Now he and his fellow engineers are being forced by events in Brussels to rethink how they construct those devices. Kirschner had just dismantled a Dell computer, as an exercise in coming to understand for himself the presence of those now undesirable chemicals that made all the connections in that machine run.

"All this [European] legislation is forcing the industry to reconsider some of the most basic production processes that have been in place for years," Kirschner said as we surveyed the wreckage on his worktable. "As an engineer, every material has a purpose. Phthalates, BPA, lead, chromium, cadmium, everything is there for a reason, for its particular properties. They work, they answer a question. Now, as we're becoming more aware of their other attributes, questions are arising as to whether they are the right answer."[15]

Kirschner chuckled nervously. "We've been in reactive hell," he said. "It's been unnerving not to be part of all these changes. Companies in this industry have been going through a twelve-step process. First step is to admit that you make electrical products." He laughs. "Then you reject that these new standards exist at all. Then you accept them. And then you adapt."

The price of not adapting was felt first at one of those critical junctures between Europe and the rest of the world: on the docks of Rotterdam, Europe's largest port. In November 2001, Dutch customs agents confiscated a shipment of 1.3 million Sony Play Stations on the Rotterdam docks. The Netherlands, one of the more densely populated countries, saw the trouble from electrical waste coming early, and in 1999 restricted the four toxic metals that would four years later be banned from all of Europe. Customs inspectors found cadmium in the Play Station cables and impounded the entire shipment on the spot. Coming at the height of the Christmas season, it was an impoundment heard around the world. *The Economist* reported that it cost the company close to one hundred million dollars in lost sales. [16]

The lost Play Stations of Rotterdam have taken on mythic status in the global electronics trade; nobody wants a repeat. "The Play Station nightmare is hanging over their head," Dr. Craig Hillman, CEO of DfR Solutions, a Maryland-based engineering consulting firm, told me six months before RoHS was to take effect.[17] U.S. industry was also, he said, acutely aware that pressure to conform to the EU's new standards would come from within their own industry—from their peers and competitors. "Other companies," he said, "will be watching and testing their [competitor's] products. Tips could find their way to authorities in Europe. That's why Dell and other big companies have a big bulls-eye on their back. . . . Competitors who spent the money to go lead-free will rat on those who did not." Thus, with prodding from the world's biggest market do the wheels of the market spin— upward for a change.

Some were caught early. In July, 2006 Apple discontinued European sales of a whole line of computer products associated with its Airport technology, as well as its entire new line of eMac computers, when it discovered that they didn't pass RoHS.[18] In the same month, the Palm company stopped shipping tens of thousands of Treo Palm Pilots to Europe for the same reasons.[19] Where would they sell them? In North America, or anywhere else in the world where the RoHS standards do not apply.

That, however, is becoming a shrinking universe. Just when U.S. producers were getting used to the idea that the action had suddenly shifted to Brussels, an elephant entered the room: China. In February 2006, China announced its own new law governing toxics in electronic equipment. It has a cumbersome name: Management

Methods for Controlling Pollution by Electronic Information Products. But it arrived like a spike in an assembly line, and is based largely on the EU's law. Mike Kirschner began expanding his consulting gigs to Shanghai and Hong Kong, to share with his China-based colleagues how international companies could adapt to China's new laws governing toxics in electronic equipment. "In some areas," he explained after returning from one of those transpacific journeys, "they're even stricter, in a few areas weaker, but in either case they're nothing like the laws we have here in the United States." Kirschner saw what most Americans have barely registered: China was moving forcefully ahead in its approach to questions of waste.

Starting in March 2007, any electronic product containing the RoHS-listed compounds must come with a label indicating the time period during which it can be used before those substances may start leaking out. A year later, all six are banned completely from all electronic products in China. This news provided a jolt to American industry, and the jolts kept coming.

By the spring of 2006, Korea, Japan, Taiwan, Canada, Australia, and Mexico announced that they would have their own laws requiring recycling and the removal of toxic substances.[20] Today, you can buy a new computer, CD player, television, or any number of thousands of electronic products and find new insignias on the bottom. They are all various versions of green circles with arrows, suggesting environmental cleanliness and recyclability; all indicate compliance with one or another of the European, Chinese, Japanese, Korean, or Taiwanese toxic-substance or recycling restrictions. There is no American equivalent.

"If you are not RoHS compliant," comments Rick Goss, environmental policy director for the Electronic Industries Alliance, "your market is evaporating as we speak."[21] The Electronics Industries Alliance (EIA), based in Washington, D.C., represents the major transnational electronics firms, with household names like Dell,

Apple, Ericsson, IBM, Microsoft, Intel, Panasonic, Sony, and Philips.

The United States is finding itself surrounded by major trading partners adopting the European Union's regulations, prompting significant changes in the industry's approach to the poisons in their products. Tech Forecasters, a high-tech consulting and design firm, estimated that the worldwide costs for implementing RoHS could amount to twenty billion dollars industry-wide over the next decade — a tiny percent of the nearly trillion-dollar-a-year global electronics trade. It's a price that Rick Goss says the industry — or at least its brand-name leaders — is willing to pay.

Goss may be one of the few corporate representatives to ever argue in favor of regulation. In the fall of 2006, he teamed up with the NGO Californians Against Waste to advocate a bill in the state legislature that actually asks that California adopt the language of Europe's RoHS, tying state law, for the first time in American history, to the law of another government. It is now pending in the state legislature.

The reasons for the EIA's turnabout are revealing. The vacuum at the federal level has prompted states to take matters into their own hands. Already New York, Maine, Massachusetts, Maryland, Washington, Illinois, and California have passed or have laws pending that are similar to RoHS, though far more limited in their scope. The prospect, said Goss, of a patchwork of different state standards was enough to unnerve major players in the industry. "We would rather have California adopt the entire RoHS directive tied to enforcement in the EU than to have the different states doing each of their own versions."

What the industry wants, he says, is a level playing field; the current situation puts the big manufacturers at a competitive disadvantage compared to companies that do not export to Europe. He calls these "white-box" manufacturers — companies without brand names that are not members of the Electronics Industry Alliance and that frequently sell through discount shops and online sites, in largely unregulated markets, like the United States. This sector of the low-end market in the United States, he said, represents from 15 to 20 percent of national electronics sales. They have not paid the costs of conforming to the European requirements, putting his members at a disadvantage. "Our industry would like to see greater harmonization," he said. The industry, he explained, "would rather have one relatively stringent global standard than sixteen or seventeen different standards." Goss went so far as to argue for such a standard in Congress in 2006, but even the industry could not convince the federal government.

In the meantime, U.S. goods now pass through a gauntlet of tests and certifications to enable them to be exported to Europe, much like American farmers must now test their crops to ensure compliance with Europe's tougher standards. The biggest industrial testing company in the world, the Swiss-based SGS, has twenty-four RoHS-certified labs: fourteen in Europe, five in China, four elsewhere in Asia, and one in the United States—in New Jersey. The company has been conducting one hundred thousand RoHS-based tests a month worldwide, according to Richard Ritchie, the company's director of business development for Restricted Substances and Testing Services.

I asked Ritchie what happens if a product fails one of his company's RoHS certification tests?

"They get dumped someplace that doesn't have the requirement," he responded.

"Where would that be?" I asked.

"The United States is in that position," Ritchie responded, "as are many other countries."[22]

A Car's Life

Jean Tinguely, a car buff, would have gotten a kick out of the New United Motor Manufacturing, Inc. (NUMMI) automobile assembly line I toured in Fremont, California. Tinguely was attracted to the Formula-1 car races for their mix of danger and sleekness and the dirty rumble of moving parts: "I like the Formula-1 because it is the most concentrated meeting between man and machine, where man and madness meet like nowhere else." He put this affection for the automobile into his art: In the 1960s, Tinguely put wheels on one of his gargantuan constructions and drove it through the center of Paris.

I wanted to see what it takes to build the defining machines of our era, and so imagined the deranged amusement Tinguely might have gotten out of sitting in the three-trailer caravan, like I did on a public tour in the winter of 2007, as we snaked through a factory run jointly by General Motors and Toyota. Spreading over the equivalent of a hundred football fields, the NUMMI plant produces Toyota Corollas, Pontiac Vibes, and Tacoma pickup trucks.

The great rolling assembly line rumbles on without end. Overhead conveyor belts carry car seats that drop one after another into Pontiac Vibe frames in red, gray, blue, and black. Nearby, in a section heavy with the smell of chemicals and grease, robots bow and rise and send off sparks as their red hot snouts weld one after another of the steel beams in the Corolla chassis. Elsewhere, pairs of workers snap tail-lights on the rear ends of passing Tacoma pickups, one a minute. The rhythm of the place is relentless—thump . . . click . . . pssstt . . . thump . . . click . . . pssstt. . . . Here was the automated construction of mobile machines—1,570 a day according to our tour guide.

Those virgin autos and trucks looked pretty impressive as they rolled off the NUMMI line, and there was an almost eerie eloquence to the precise steps at every stage of the process that got them there.

But all is not so smooth inside the two companies that produce them, or with their U.S.-based competitors. Both GM and Toyota, along with Ford, Chrysler, and Honda, were party to a lawsuit seeking to overturn a California law requiring vehicles to produce 30 percent less greenhouse gas emissions than today's models, by 2016—goals that are roughly equivalent to emission restrictions that came into force in Europe following implementation of the Kyoto treaty. And while car engineers have long faced an array of different national standards they must meet to sell in different national markets—from specifications for things like the installation of seat belts to the wattage of a taillight—for the first time they are now facing questions from Europe about the construction materials within. Every year such aging or disposed-of cars create more than twenty million tons of waste across the United States and Europe.

Europe is now doing to cars what it has done to electronics: insisting on similar life-cycle production and disposal practices by the manufacturers. The philosophically titled End of Life Vehicles Directive, or ELV, requires that all cars produced or sold in the EU be built with at least 80 percent, by weight, of "recyclable components"; by 2015 that figure rises to 85 percent. ELV further requires that manufacturers take responsibility for disposing of their cars—a powerful incentive to reach those goals of recyclable materials. The directive also bans the use of four toxic heavy metals that have long been prevalent in cars: cadmium, chromium, mercury, and lead.[23] The automobile industry was being forced to look warily toward Europe, just as its peers in the electronics industry were doing.

"We've been hit by a tsunami," is how Michael Taubitz, the Global Health and Safety Regulatory Liaison for General Motors, put it to me from his office outside Detroit. Taubitz has been an engineer at GM for forty-one years; he started working at an engine plant in Flint, Michigan, and now, as the company's representative on the Health and Safety Steering Committee of the Auto Industry

Action Group, he leads their efforts to keep pace with the multiplicity of new standards affecting his industry.[24]

General Motors, of course, was long considered the very epitome of American dynamism and leadership. "What's good for General Motors," the saying went, "is good for America." Today, however, the company is sensing its loss of control over the new forces emanating from Europe, that dictate what goes in under the hood. "The End of Life Vehicles Directive came washing over us in 2003," Taubitz said, "and we had an immediate multibillion dollar problem."

Taubitz was frank in describing how dramatically the landscape had shifted underneath the mighty foundation once laid by the U.S. car industry. In the 1990s, he explained, GM prided itself on developing a globally harmonized production structure. Those cars in Fremont, for example, were being built with chassis from Mexico, engines from Japan, and electrical consoles from Canada. "We made ourselves into a truly 'global' company," he said. "Back in the nineties, we were enthusiastic about global harmonization. In those days, the view in the industry was, 'Okay, fine, so everything will be built along American lines.'"

The problem, of course, came when the global transmission shifted gears. "What we did not anticipate," he said, "was how leadership in defining the regulatory parameters for our industry would shift from the United States to Europe. . . . It used to be that every time the EPA came forward with a new regulation, industry would hammer them down. But now those regulations are coming out of Europe, they're the ones driving the train."[25] A train over which neither GM nor any other American car company has significant influence — certainly not on par with the influence it wields in the United States.

For a sense of the challenges now faced by the industry, Taubitz referred me to something called the Global Automotive Declarable Substance List (GADSL). This obscure list was created by the Auto Industry Action Group, a consortium of car companies created to assist with regulatory and other challenges common to all in the industry. "GADSL is used to enhance further dialogue and cooperation along the supply chain on the benefits and potential risks of certain substances or groups of substances in a specified use within vehicles parts/materials," reads the action group's explanation for the list. Despite the bland language, the list provides a glimpse into the chemical insides of an automobile, and a sense of how absent the United States has been in regulating them. It is intended to offer manufacturers guidance as to what substance is acceptable where. GADSL includes thirty-one chemicals that are either banned or restricted for use in cars, a collection of carcinogens, neural disrupters, and acutely toxic chemicals ranging from amines used in seat and rug dyes to flame-retarding PBDEs to vinyl chloride used in interiors. Twenty-seven of the thirty-one chemicals on the list cite restrictions or outright bans by the European Union. Just four cite U.S. law, all of them chlorofluorocarbons, substances that are governed under the restrictions of the Montreal Protocol, to which the United States and Europe are parties.[26]

U.S. car companies export few cars to Europe; thus, U.S. manufacturers are under little direct pressure to adapt to European standards. But each of the American "big three" has substantial ties to the European market: Ford has its own Ford Europe production facilities, and owns the Jaguar line in the UK; General Motors owns the German Opel, the Swedish Saab, and produces its own line of vehicles in the UK under the Vauxhall label; until May 2007, when it was sold to the U.S. firm Cerberus Capital Managment, Chrysler was owned by the German manufacturer Daimler-Benz. Each of these companies has established state-of-the-art scrap yards for breaking their product down in Europe, and has reformulated their production lines to abide by the new chemical restrictions established by the EU, and embodied in the GADSL guidelines.

But there are few signs that companies making cars for the U.S.

market are removing the chemicals from U.S. autos that they have removed from their European counterparts. The idea of taking responsibility for the "take back" of old cars has never even been proposed on a federal level because of the opposition of the car industry.

"I have not seen anything in the United States like the recycling we're doing here in the UK or in Europe," commented David Hutton, who oversees U.S. automobile regulations for InterReg, Ltd., a British firm that provides regulatory-status reports from around the world to the automobile and other industries.[27]

Martha Bucknell, executive director of the Auto Dismantlers Association in California, said that she had never heard of GADSL, and had seen no changes in the content of automobiles that her membership uses to rebuild old cars or sell for scrap.[28]

Back in Brussels, Rosalinde van der Vlies, who helped to oversee the ELV as part of her job in the Environment Directorate, told me that Japanese and Korean car companies were already adapting to the ELV directives requirements. In 2006 the Association of South-East Asian Nations issued a policy recommendation that all of Southeast Asia apply similar policies among its membership. Japan already has laws very closely hewing to the guidelines laid down by the European Union. As for the United States, Taubitz explained, "We conform to European regulations in Europe, to Brazilian regulations in Brazil, to French regulations in France, and to U.S. regulations in the United States."

Thus, in some instances, like electronics, Americans are actually beneficiaries of Europe's attempt to raise the environmental bar; in others, Americans are finding themselves with fewer protections than their foreign counterparts and exposed to substances from which increasing numbers of people around the world are being protected. In the next chapter, we will see how the new forces unleashed by globalization may leave the United States with little choice but to adapt to the rising consciousness about environmental risk.

7

Chemical Revolution

Human Test Dummies

One drizzly fall morning in Brussels, I followed a troupe of women on a visit to the European Parliament. They were a motley gathering of three generations from thirteen families—grandmothers, mothers, and daughters—making their way through the vast chambers of the Parliament's Spinelli Building. Altiero Spinelli, a political prisoner under the Italian dictator Benito Mussolini, later emerged as an eloquent advocate of a united Europe and is now remembered in that modernist building of steel and glass where most of the members of the European Parliament have their offices. The women came from France, Germany, Hungary, Italy, Greece and seven other countries across Europe, and were selected by the World Wildlife Fund International to have their blood tested for 107 different chemicals. They came to the Parliament, much like Americans go to Congress, to demand that their representatives act on the chemical risks that they confront every day.

Unlike a Tinguely machine, we humans are blessed with considerable power to influence the terms of our mortality. We introduce variation and toy with one or another of the factors that can speed the course of the inevitable. Smoke? Drink? Fly in an airplane? Drive a car? Run across the railroad tracks as a train approaches? It's called risk. We calculate the odds and make a deal with fate. We have, in short, information as to the consequences of these actions, and we decide. Just up the road from the Parliament, on the other side of the Parc Leopold, the Berlaymont had undergone a thirteen-year restoration when asbestos was found floating out of the walls and ceilings into the offices of European commissioners and their staff. The entire commission was put into temporary quarters from 1991 until 2004, when the billion-dollar cleanup and renovation was completed. Regarding asbestos' potent carcinogenicity, a worldwide consensus had emerged from scientific research and from internal company tests pried free through legal action in Europe and in the United States (though the United States, unlike Europe, has yet to actually ban asbestos; more on that later). However, regarding most other chemicals, those to which we are exposed daily in everyday consumer products, there is little such information. The women in the Parliament that day wanted to increase their odds against those hidden chemical risks.

All of the women looked vigorous and healthy, except for the intravenous stands rattling alongside them. Carrying these props of illness, the women passed through the Parliament like some specter of mortality from the world outside—which of course was the point. Members of Parliament hustled past, harried aides bustled alongside with cell phones glued to their ears, television cameras caught interviews on the fly; the multigenerational tableau served as a jarring reminder of how quickly the robustness of health can turn into its opposite. From each intravenous stand dangled a plasma bag filled with the blood from their bodies. Or it was meant to look like blood

anyway. The World Wildlife Fund had chosen to test three generations because, according to the group's bio-monitoring coordinator,
Karl Wagner, "there's nothing more powerful than the family."[1]

Blood doesn't lie. The largest number of chemicals—sixty-three—
was found in the group of grandmothers. Given the length of time
they had to accumulate exposure over the course of a lifetime, that
perhaps was not surprising. The surprise, however, was that the next
highest level was among their grandchildren, aged eleven to twenty,
who were discovered to have accumulated fifty-nine different toxic
chemicals in their short lifetimes. The biggest chemical load had
skipped a generation—their mothers had forty-nine. Many of the
chemicals were known by authorities in Europe and the United
States to be possible contributors to cancer, neurological dysfunction,
and possibly disruptive effects on the reproductive systems of the
women still of childbearing age. Offspring of the women who came
of age during the birth of the environmental movement—when
awareness of unseen toxic triggers was just beginning—were showing
exposure to a greater number of chemicals than their mothers.[2]

The nature and amount of the chemicals found in the daughters
was different from those found in their grandmothers. The former
had more brominated flame retardants (PBDEs), the potential neurotoxin used to coat many electronic and other devices that the POPS
signatories are trying to ban from the world, and more of the plastic
additive bisphenol A, suspected of mimicking estrogen and being carcinogenic. Wagner said the abundance of those substances was
clearly a symptom of the modern proliferation of plastic. The grandmothers had more residues of pesticides and old industrial chemicals
like polychlorinated biphenyls, which continue to show up in people,
wildlife, and soil years after they were banned in Europe (and the
United States) for their carcinogenic and neurotoxic effects. Clearly,
chemicals were finding their generational niche.

I watched in the Parliament's cafeteria as the women presented their concerns to a group of MEPs. A Greek member of the delegation, Kalliopi Vogiatzi of Athens, said that what really disturbed her was discovering that her daughter, whom she had left back home in Athens because it was a school day, had more chemicals in her blood than she did. That, Vogiatzi said, was enough to prompt her to take three days off from her job as an assistant pharmacist and travel to Brussels. "What am I supposed to do with my daughter?" she exclaimed. "I'm forty, she's twelve. I can't put her in a glass to protect her!"[3]

Afterward, I sat down with Eleonora Bruno, a nineteen-year-old Italian. She'd come to Brussels from Bari, Italy, along with her mother and grandmother. If not for the intravenous stand by her side, and the plasma sac full of red "blood" dangling overhead, Ms. Bruno would have looked like any other teenager, robust and energetic. Her blond hair was brushed down over a black T-shirt that read, in bold white letters: De-Tox Me. There was no hint that Bruno's heart was pumping toxins through her body along with the normal bounty of life-giving nutrients. Yet they were there, as if she had just drunk them in a soda.

The twenty-four chemicals she had discovered in her blood included PBDEs, PCBs, and organochlorine pesticides like DDT and a derivative of lindane, that pesticide which Mexico had put on the POPS list of environmental war criminals. Others she discovered: a family of perfluorinated chemicals that are used as stain and water repellents for clothing and furniture and in nonstick cookware, and are known carcinogens; and artificial musk aromas contained in perfumes and soaps made from a synthetic substance called galaxolide, that scientists claim can reduce the ability of the body to expel other toxins.

Ms. Bruno had spoken with her doctor back in Italy about her chemical burden, and the doctor had shared her concerns of declining fertility rates among many women she was seeing, and their possible links to chemical exposure. "It was not a pleasure to discover this," she said. She has been studying chemistry at the university in

Bari in the hopes of becoming a biologist, and so is coming to understand how chemicals work with one another and within the body. She had just taken an exam in her chemistry class. "My first exam was about how the cells work in order to create the human body," she told me. "After that exam, I really appreciated what endocrine disrupters are, and how they work."[4]

We subsequently engaged in an ongoing e-mail dialogue, in which Ms. Bruno expressed her rising frustration as her knowledge of chemicals increased. She wrote of the mystifying double life of chemicals in the just slightly imperfect English that can humble any of us who have tried to actually write in a foreign language. "These brominated flame retardants they found in my blood, they are sneaky," she wrote. "They have been created to protect us from accidental blazes of domestic appliances and furniture. Actually, they are bio-accumulative, and they can provoke behavioral changes, they are endocrine disrupters. A high percentage of nonstick perfluorinated chemicals were also found in my and my mother's blood. Where can you find them? In the notorious Teflon pans. You cook peacefully, but actually you are getting a stab in the back! In fact they have been linked to liver damage and can lead to an increased risk of bladder and possibly other cancers. What scared me more when I saw the results was the existence of these 'false friends': They should help us, but they damage us."[5]

Later I called Ms. Bruno's doctor, Donatella Caserta, who is director of the physiology and pathology unit at the Center for Human Reproduction at the University of Rome; she had volunteered to consult with the World Wildlife Fund in Italy. Dr. Caserta would not address Ms. Bruno's individual health status—citing, as would any doctor, rules of confidentiality. (It had been Ms. Bruno herself who sent me her own exposure report by e-mail after we'd met in Brussels. In the World Wildlife Funds's report, De-Tox, code numbers identify the families.)

Dr. Caserta told me that it is difficult to predict what precise effects those chemicals might have on Ms. Bruno or anybody else carrying such a toxic burden (meaning, most of us). But what is clear is that chemicals interact with the body in multifarious ways: Some have similar molecular structures to the body's own hormones and insinuate themselves directly into the endocrine system; they mimic the body's own natural chemical messengers. Others lodge in the hospitable environment of fatty tissue; petrochemicals, those substances made from a petroleum base, penetrate the oil-based membranes of the cells. However their mode of entry, once in the body they may wreak their destructive powers, often in concert with other synthetic substances, decades from now. Or they may not. There is much we still don't know about how chemicals work in the body, but scientists have been able to identify their potentially toxic effects, and symptoms that would be consistent with those effects.

Caserta oversees a research division at the hospital that investigates how chemicals act in the bodies of young adults. "What we know," she said, "is that we're seeing chemicals that are not an integral part of our body. We know we are seeing higher rates of infertility, lower sperm counts, reproductive-system distortions. We know that there is evidence suggesting chemicals can act as endocrine disrupters. We know that the amount of these types of chemicals is rising in the blood. What we need to know now is what the real action these substances are having on the human body."[6] The fears now, of scientists like Caserta and others, are the effects that may be seen over time from extremely low doses, measured in parts per million or even parts per billion. This signifies a dramatic shift in the science of toxicology, which has traditionally assessed chemical risk on the basis of volume: the higher the quantity of a potentially dangerous chemical, the higher the risk. Recent evidence suggests an unexpected twist in this assessment: some chemicals may have an effect only at low doses, while higher doses may trigger receptors to shut down, or trigger an immune reaction that is not triggered by the far more common low-dose exposures.[7]

What has been discovered in the blood of Europeans has its almost perfect echo in what is also being discovered in Americans. Shortly after the women's visit to Brussels, the Center for Disease Control's National Survey on Family Growth concluded that the fastest growing segment of the population with "impaired fecundity"—i.e., infertility, an inability to conceive of or carry a child—is women under the age of twenty-five,[8] Eleonora Bruno's age group. Many scientists speculated that the infertility spike could be due, at least partly, to the abundance of chemicals to which the group is exposed: neither genetics nor lifestyle is enough on its own to explain the jump. The CDC itself had released findings in 2005 from a comprehensive survey of Americans dispersed across the population who were registering the presence of at least 148 chemicals in their blood,[9] a similar chemical mix to that which had been found in the blood of Europeans.

In 2005 and 2006 it seemed as if an iridescent light was shining from all those hidden ingredients now circulating in our veins. The Environmental Working Group conducted tests on the umbilical cords of ten infants and discovered the presence of likely carcinogenic, endocrine-disrupting, and neurotoxic chemicals that passed from mothers to their developing fetuses through the placenta.[10] Among them were the perfluorinated substances used in nonstick cookware and plastic packaging, and those PBDE flame retardants that Europe had proposed banning at the POPS conference. One could easily imagine that in nineteen years those infants would have a similar toxic load to that of Eleonora Bruno today. Greenpeace UK released a study showing chemicals in the umbilical cord blood of European infants, many of the same chemicals that had been seen in American infants;[11] Italian politicians agreed to have their blood monitored by scientists associated with Greenpeace Italy; citizens of

Washington State were found by the Toxic Free Legacy Coalition to have levels of chemical residue approaching and/or exceeding levels that the EPA terms "safe."[12] The veteran journalist Bill Moyers had samples taken for a documentary, *Trade Secrets*, and discovered 84 chemical substances in his blood, including dioxins, PCBs, and the endocrine-disrupting phthalate DEHP.[13] I myself had a strand of hair analyzed for mercury, at a booth sponsored by the Harvard School of Public Health during a conference of the Society of Environmental Journalists—and discovered it was on the low end of high concern.

It was a season for getting acquainted with our bodies' synthetic cocktail, and the evidence in our blood tells the story: we are marinating in a chemical soup. Chemicals, it turns out, are being tested—on us, in real time. Bio-monitoring enables us to understand how we are the "blind" in this grand experiment, an experiment in which there is no comparative "control." And while exposure levels are essentially the same on both sides of the Atlantic, there is far more than an ocean of difference in the response.

Fall & Rise of the Environmental Mohicans

Since the end of World War II, molecules thrown together in heretofore unheard of combinations have given rise to new products inconceivable a couple of generations ago. Those nonstick substances, for example, have added new levels of convenience, and those polybrominated flame retardants have certainly reduced the chance of fire. But like the luster of technology that was slowly fading inside those four walls of the Atomium, what was being found in our circulatory systems also offered a glimpse into the legacy left behind by the inventiveness of the chemical age. The chemical imprints in our blood have prompted a reassessment, in Europe, of chemistry's magic.

For a quarter-century, the Bruno family and other Europeans have relied on principles of regulation based substantially on those of the United States for their protection from chemical hazards. The Toxic Substances Control Act, or TSCA, was passed by Congress in 1976, six years after President Richard Nixon created the EPA. TSCA was the first effort by any government to attempt to assert some level of oversight over the vast amount of chemicals that had been introduced into the marketplace since the end of World War II. The new law took effect in 1977. In those days environmental policy in Europe was largely in the hands of individual governments. TSCA had the effect of prompting the continent's major chemical powers—West Germany, France, and the UK—to harmonize their varying regulations to conform more closely to those of TSCA. The rest of the European Community's then-nine other members quickly followed.[14]

TSCA's primary innovation at the time was in requiring that all chemicals developed from that point on be subject to review for their toxicity before reaching the market. That sounds good, except for one major caveat: TSCA exempted all chemicals already on the market from review. The EPA made up a list of all chemicals already for sale as of December 1979 and called it the TSCA Inventory. Some sixty-two thousand chemicals were grandfathered into the market, with no testing or review. These included thousands of potentially highly toxic substances, including the likes of ethyl benzene, a widely used industrial solvent suspected of being a potent neurotoxin; whole families of synthetic plastics that are potential carcinogens and endocrine disrupters; and thousands of other substances for which there was little or no information.

Twenty-eight years later, according to the EPA itself, 95 percent of all chemicals have never undergone even minimal testing for their toxicity or environmental impact. Researchers at the University of California–Berkeley's School of Public Health estimate that forty-two billion pounds of chemicals enter American commerce daily—enough chemicals to fill up 623,000 tanker trucks every day, a string of trucks that could straddle the United States twice if placed end to end.[15] The EPA has required testing on fewer than 200 of those substances.[16]

Even for those few new chemicals that industry does bring to market, the record is not reassuring. The EPA requires that a pre-market notification be supplied for the agency's review ninety days before commercial-scale manufacturing of new chemicals begins. Manufacturers are supposed to include production volume, intended uses, and available exposure and toxicity data. Theoretically, this permits the Office of Pollution Prevention and Toxics to determine whether regulatory action is warranted before the chemicals hit the market. But according to their own figures, 85 percent of the notifications submitted annually contain no health data.[17]

There has been abundant criticism of inadequacies in TSCA for more than two decades. A legion of non-governmental organizations, scientists, and even government agencies has been devoted to advocating TSCA's reform. The Government Accountability Office concluded in 2005 that the agency has inadequate test data to make safety assessments, and has permitted the chemical industry too much leeway in keeping information from public view by indiscriminate assertion of proprietary information. The requirements that the EPA include the "costs to industry" in determining whether a substance presents an "unreasonable threat to public health," and that it impose the "least burdensome regulation" (to industry) was a bar that the GOA found too high for effective protection from chemicals' potential harm.[18] One result of these rules was that the EPA has banned just five chemicals since the agency's creation a quarter century ago. There was, briefly, a sixth substance on the EPA's banned list: asbestos. In 1989, the EPA declared a ban on what amounted to more than 90 percent of all uses of asbestos, which it classified as a "known carcinogen." But industry challenged the agency and in 1991 a federal court vacated the ban, asserting that the EPA had not met TSCA's requirements for proof of harm balanced against the benefits

of asbestos, and had not demonstrated that the ban was the "least burdensome alternative" for eliminating the "unreasonable risk" of exposure to the carcinogenic substance.[19] More than thirty million pounds
of asbestos is still sold in the United States each year, used as insula-
tion in an array of products including brake shoes and industrial tiles.
The agency has not acted to ban a chemical since that decision.

One of TSCA's most significant weaknesses, according to Joseph
Guth, a biochemist and lawyer who works as legal director of the
Science and Environmental Health Network, is that by making it
easier to hang onto old chemicals rather than develop new ones, it
provides no incentive for developing less toxic alternatives. "TSCA
rewards ignorance," Guth said. "The chemical companies give you
function and they give you price. What they don't give you is safety
or environmental effects. That is a complete black box. The data
gaps are massive. So, let's say you want to develop a more effective
and safer chemical. There is no information out there to prove that
yours is better or safer for human health or the environment. There's
no competitive pressure to improve it. . . . The current system
impedes the ability of innovations to penetrate the market."[20]
Consumers, in other words, have no means of expressing their potential preference for less toxic alternatives.

The Nobel Prize–winning economist Joseph Stiglitz called this
inequality of knowledge between consumers and producers "information asymmetry," and pegged it as one of the central flaws of market
capitalism.[21] The absence of even minimal toxicity data works to insu-
late the industry from the normal supply-demand dynamic of the
market. In a country that prides itself on its entrepreneurial ingenuity,
the United States is hitching its faith to a system that reinforces stasis
and a potentially dangerous status quo.

The bio-monitoring results in America and in Europe are the
clinching evidence of TSCA's ineffectiveness. "All our exposure
assumptions have been proven wrong," Malcolm Woolf, staff

counsel to the Senate Environment and Public Works Committee, told me. "Because we did not act under TSCA, the assumption is that chemicals have been certified safe. But it's exactly the opposite: they haven't been certified anything."[22] TSCA is now derisively referred to among its many critics as the "Toxic Substances Conversation Act." The chemical industry has wielded considerable power in Washington to keep it that way. Over the past decade, the industry has been either the second or third biggest lobbying force on Capitol Hill, according to the Center for Responsive Politics. Between 1996 and 2006, the industry made $35 million in contributions to federal election campaigns, and spends between $2 million and $5 million each year on lobbying in Washington (not including the significant amount of lobbying by the industry in state capitals).[23]

Lynn Goldman, a pediatrician and epidemiologist, served as assistant administrator for the EPA's Office of Prevention, Pesticides and Toxic Substances from 1993 to 1998, when she left to become a professor of environmental health sciences at the Bloomberg School of Public Health at Johns Hopkins University. By the mid-1990s, she told me, the flaws in TSCA had become abundantly clear. "Suddenly all of us were realizing, there were thousands of chemicals out there, and we didn't know what they were. We weren't able to get the data, weren't able to assess the risks, nothing." Goldman recalls a party held in Washington in 1996 to celebrate TSCA's twenty-year anniversary. "I'll never forget. Someone from the chemical industry got up to salute TSCA, and said, 'This is the perfect statute. I wish every law could be like TSCA.'" She laughed, "It was then I knew for sure there was something wrong."[24]

The act's long reign, however, is about to end. The United States hardly needed a foreign hand to set its downfall into motion, but that's what happened. TSCA's demise, and with it American preeminence in environmental protection, was set into motion by a series of alarming news reports in Europe.

Chemical Reaction

In the late 1990s, newspapers in Denmark and the Netherlands reported that infants were being routinely exposed to carcinogens and neurotoxins. Babies were sleeping in pajamas treated with poly-brominated flame retardants; they were sucking on bottles laced with phthalate-containing polyvinyl chloride; their diapers were glued together with tributyltin, a neurotoxin normally used to line the bottom of ships to kill algae. The same chemical, it would later be revealed in German newspapers, was used in the jerseys of Germany's national soccer team.

The stories spread across Europe as reporters picked up the local angle. Revelations of children's exposure to toxins sparked demonstrations by angry mothers and fathers in London, Copenhagen, the Hague, Brussels, and elsewhere demanding action against the poisons that seemed to be hiding in full sight. But when health officials began following the trail of baby products, they were confounded by how little they actually knew about the chemicals inside. Regulators discovered that they did not possess the information needed to control potential hazards from the thousands of chemicals with which all Europeans, not only infants, come into contact over the course of a lifetime. Some of the manufacturers did not even know what was in their own products. The great black hole at the heart of TSCA and its European cousins was laid bare.

"There was great political anxiety in Europe when we discovered that carcinogenic and bio-accumulative chemicals were being released from consumer products like diapers, from softeners in baby toys, and then from the jerseys of German soccer players," Robert Donkers recalled. By mimicking the body's own hormones or lodging in fatty tissues, bio-accumulative chemicals are generally not expelled through the normal excretion mechanisms of the human body; instead, they "accumulate" inside the body, releasing their toxins slowly, over time.

"We discovered that neither consumers nor the government was informed about the chemical properties of what is in those and other products and how they break down," Donkers said. "An overhaul was needed."[25] Donkers was put in charge of the overhaul.

Few Europeans anticipated how deeply that overhaul would strike at the status quo. Industry and trade experts were called in to assess how business would be affected by any proposals. Talks between the two sides were tense as the Europeans faced head-on the tensions between industrial competitiveness and consumer protection. "Negotiations were a bloodbath," recalled Andrew Fasey, a Briton who frequently sat across from Donkers at those meetings, as a representative of the Industry Directorate, Europe's equivalent of the Department of Commerce.[26] The more they probed, the more contentious the meetings became, and the more they discovered how central chemicals had become to the modern economy.

After four years of deliberation, in October 2003 the European Commission issued its proposal. They called it REACH, for Registration, Evaluation, and Authorization of Chemicals. REACH's primary target was that enormous TSCA loophole. It would, for the first time, secure environmental- and health-toxicity data on the more than sixty thousand untested chemicals grandfathered into the market. Chemicals would have to be "registered," "evaluated," and "authorized" before being permitted to remain on the market. For those deemed a "potentially significant threat to human health or the environment," —carcinogens, mutagens, or reproductive toxins— specific approval would be required and conditions for use imposed. In addition to substances in their raw form, REACH also extended to consumer products that utilized chemicals—thus tens of thousands of "downstream users," from construction companies to tennis-shoe manufacturers to fashion houses to the creators of synthetic aromas, would be impelled to pay attention to the collateral effects of the substances used in their products.

The proposal flipped the American presumption of innocent until proven guilty on its head, by placing the burden of proof on manufacturers to demonstrate that their chemicals could be used safely. And REACH proposed to limit the amount of health-related data that companies could claim was "proprietary," and to release that information on the European Chemical Agency's Web site—making it available to Americans as well. "We realized," Donkers said, "that we were taking on the chemical establishment."[27]

Europe was about to become the vanguard in a transatlantic environmental battle. Globalization was shaking up traditional patterns of influence in everything from music to manufacturing. I interviewed Bo Manderup Jensen, a Dane who is the European Commission's chief liaison to the European Parliament (in America he would be a White House congressional relations officer), in his office in the upper floors of the Spinelli Building, who was intent on explaining how fundamentally the European Union was transforming the old imperatives of the single nation-state. The EU itself, with twenty-seven countries voluntarily entwining their political and economic fates, exemplifies this change. "National sovereignty," Jensen said, "lasts for, oh, about five seconds. That's the length of time it takes for news from the Bundesbank to be transmitted to financial markets around the world." News of interest rates in Frankfurt, he suggested, could shake up economic planning instantaneously in New York, Tokyo, and around the world.[28] Americans would soon learn that environmental principles could be subject to similar, though far slower, shake-ups emanating from Brussels.

REACH, though, would take more than three years before coming to a final vote. First the Europeans' attempt to reform a global industry would jump-start lobbying on a global scale never seen before.

———

While REACH was being hotly debated in Europe, U.S. industry had little to worry about in Washington. By mid-decade, EPA administrator Christine Todd-Whitman was chopping up the authority of what had once been the world's premier agency for environmental protection. Whitman had overseen a 5 percent decrease in the EPA's annual budget since 2001; had loosened restrictions on toxic releases into the air and water; had taken major elements of its mercury exposure rules from industry position papers (according to the EPA's own inspector general); had appointed industry lobbyists to sensitive positions overseeing toxic chemicals; had cut the agency's enforcement division by 12 percent; had reduced the number of fines assessed for environmental violations to an all-time low; and was subjecting proposed regulations to ever-more severe cost-benefit analyses and ever-more aggressive industry input. The EPA's evisceration from within was prompting a flurry of midlevel professionals to flee the agency.

The traffic in chemicals moves in as many directions as the global economy itself. Europe is the world's largest chemical producer, controlling about 33 percent of the global market, compared to the United States' 28 percent. U.S. firms sell about $27 billion a year in chemicals to Europe; European firms sell about $41 billion in chemicals to the United States.[29] Dozens of other countries sell Europe millions of tons of raw chemicals, not to mention chemical-containing consumer goods. Europe's trade interactions are as diverse as America's. Just as TSCA set the international standard for the previous century, REACH was set to be the new international standard for the twenty-first century. From Bangalore to Beijing to Boston, manufacturers around the world would be subject to REACH's new toxicity screening requirements if they wanted to sell in Europe.

Nicolas Thery, a senior lawyer on trade issues with the Internal Markets Directorate, whose mandate is to maintain open markets between EU member states (much like the U.S. Interstate Commerce Commission ensures that American states do not create obstacles to commerce with other states), explained to me that Europe's pushing of the REACH initiative evolved as the EU itself grew more cognizant of the political power that comes with rising economic force. Thery, a Frenchman with an energetic passion for the power plays that lurk just behind the arcane details of trade law, had worked with Pascal Lamy, who was the director general for trade before taking his current position as director of the World Trade Organization.

"I was in DG Trade back when the GE merger with Honeywell was blocked," Thery told me. "That was in 2001. Even in Europe, that was perceived as some kind of fluke, like the guy in the soccer game who accidentally kicks the ball into his own net. But it was not. This was not a mistake." It was the first time the EU wielded the political muscle that goes with its economic power. And it worked; no financial cataclysm followed. General Electric adjusted its plans and is still deeply involved in the European market through its numerous subsidiaries. And European principles of fair competition grew stronger, as Microsoft would discover four years later. REACH, Thery continued, "is the test case for us."[30]

Europe is aware that the big conflicts today are over who writes the rules, the values that underlie them, and who listens. "Trade is not about a bunch of chickens and tomatoes," he said. "The big issues in the world now are questions of standards and regulations. This is now the huge debate. In Europe, there has always been this protest over 'American imperialism.' Now Americans finally cannot believe that there might be what they think is 'EU imperialism' when it comes to setting those standards."

Shortly after my meeting with Nicolas Thery, I had dinner with Robert Donkers, when he was back in Brussels for a visit to the home office. We met at Balthazar, a restaurant just down the block from the Berlaymont, a popular refuge for Eurocrats seeking a quiet place to cut deals amid the muted yellow walls and plush banquettes. The Washington equivalent might be some establishment like the Monocle, which for over nearly fifty years has provided a high-end destination for dealmakers down the block from the U.S. Senate—except Balthazar has been in Brussels for barely a decade, its reputation for power meals coinciding with the EU's own rising engagement in global affairs.

Donkers is a bit of a gourmand, and a complete fan of American jazz. He plays jazz and blues guitar during his rare off-hours. Now, with four years in Washington under his belt, Donkers had been able to indulge his love of American music and enthused about a Dave Brubeck concert he had seen back in the States. He had been traveling the country, and had become an aficionado of the great, open American landscapes and "the entrepreneurial energy" that a European can't help but notice among Americans. He even confessed to preferring, now and again, the wines of California to those of the French, his fellow Europeans. Tonight, though, to go with his filet mignon—"rare!"—he ordered a Bordeaux.

Donkers' unusual diplomatic mandate gives him a foot on either side of the Atlantic; he has become a popular fixture at U.S. industry conferences, explaining what the EU is up to, and why. He is still mystified, he says, at what Americans don't understand about their own system. "The assumption among Americans is, 'If it's on the market, it's okay,'" he said. "Dream on. That fantasy is gone in Europe. We're asking the question: Why should the government be in the position of proving that something is not safe? But in the United States, there's still a level of confidence that if there is a problem, the government would do something about it and the chemical wouldn't be there. That's the fallacy. That it's safe." Donkers sipped his Boudreaux. "I beg to differ."

"You have to ask this question: 'On the basis of what is it safe'? More than sixty thousand chemicals were grandfathered into the market by TSCA. We don't know anything about them. Are they safe or are they not safe? They are still here because they were already here. We are learning this now in Europe." U.S. companies, he warned, could be put at a serious competitive disadvantage if they did not acknowledge the changes coming down the line. He cut into his filet mignon. "You're either helping draft the menu," he said, "or you're on it."[31]

What the Europeans saw as a means of protecting their citizens also presented an unparalleled opportunity for U.S. consumers. REACH would put chemicals that have undergone toxic screening in Europe into open competition with American chemicals that have not been screened. Not only would chemicals be subject to their first-ever toxic review, but also the findings would be published on the Web. What Americans were unable to obtain from their own government would be accessible online from the European Chemicals Bureau in Helsinki.

"If people in Europe don't have chemicals in their products that are dangerous, maybe we don't want those same chemicals in our products either," commented Charlotte Brody, the nurse who is executive director of Commonweal, an environmental health research institute in California. "The chemical industry is scared that the American people might not want to be second-class world citizens."[32]

This was a door that neither U.S. industry nor the Bush administration wanted opened. "Industry and the administration don't like REACH because they fear that environmental actors around the world could use that toxicity data to demand replacement of hazardous chemicals in their own countries," commented Stacy Vandeveer, a professor of political science at Brown University's Watson Institute for International Studies.[33] A record of the minutes of a joint State and Commerce Department "Roundtable on Transatlantic Standards," held in January 2005 with chemical, cosmetics, automobile, and other industry officials, revealed rising anxiety over the "de facto international standards" being promoted by the EU, and the "alarming . . . dichotomy" between European and American environmental regulations.[34] While the American public was largely unaware of these developments, U.S. industry was becoming painfully aware, jolted from the easy presumption that the locus of power influencing their future was in Washington. An international campaign was launched to kill the proposed regulation before it became law.

Making of a Transatlantic Lobby

According to the Amsterdam-based Corporate European Observatory, there are fifteen thousand registered lobbyists in Brussels today; of those, more than one third were not there at the turn of the century.[35] The influence business is going global as the EU's rise gives lobbyists reason to travel. The biggest non-European contingent is American. Hundreds of American lobbyists left the familiar corridors of Washington behind and set up shop around the Rond Point Schuman in the heart of the EU district of southeast Brussels. To the north of the Rond Point is the expanse of royal gardens in the Parc du Centainaire, where the figure of King Leopold I sits on horseback looking straight down the Boulevard Arts et Loi toward the source of European power in the Berlaymont. The king never could have imagined what an international hothouse his beloved Brussels, capital of tiny Belgium, has become. Many of the American players who hit Brussels with hopes of derailing REACH made their new home in Leopold's shadow along these broad avenues.

The Brussels offices of Dow and DuPont are a five-minute walk from the Environment, Enterprise, and Internal Market Directorates. Other Washington transplants are in the neighborhood too: Burson-Marsteller, which has been working on behalf of the

American Chemical Council; APCO, where former undersecretary of commerce Stuart Eisenstadt took a job after leaving the Clinton administration and began making regular visits to top European officials, like Nicolas Thery, to argue against REACH; and Hill & Knowlton, which has been representing DuPont along with dozens of other U.S. companies. On the other side of the EU district, abutting the European Parliament off the Place Leopold, is AmCham EU, the most active lobbying house on behalf of U.S. multinationals operating in Europe.

In 2000 the U.S. Chamber of Commerce in Brussels changed its name to AmCham EU and expanded its staff to reflect the new realities of the single European market. AmCham EU lobbies the parliament and commission in Brussels on behalf of its 140 members, U.S. companies including Boeing, Dow, DuPont, Apple, General Motors, American Express, and Cargill. Environmental policies top their list of concerns. "Every single one of the companies we represent is touched by REACH," explained AmCham EU's Belgian spokesperson, Anja Duchuteau. "[Our companies] have to comply with whoever sets the most severe regulations. Whoever sets those establishes the standards for the rest of the world. And a lot of those standards are now coming out of Brussels."[36]

Joe Mayhew, a chemical industry lobbyist for the American Chemical Council, expressed to me how his industry had been confounded by new laws and regulations emanating from Brussels and a system with which, until recently, it was utterly unfamiliar: "We used to have to deal with individual countries," he said. "We'd pay attention to, say, France. Not to be pejorative here, but we wouldn't really pay much attention to what Spain was doing. Having the EU as a single bloc with regulatory authority is a new thing for us."[37] The chemical industry would soon have the support of that other major lobbying player in town, the U.S. Mission to the European Union.

While Americans watched the buildup of military forces preparing for the invasion of Iraq, the administration declared war on REACH. Defense Secretary Donald Rumsfeld's immortal words denouncing the irrelevance of "old Europe" to U.S. policy came just as "old Europe" was causing anxiety in the State Department. A position paper, circulated inside the Bureau of European Affairs, denounced REACH as too "costly, burdensome and complex" for industry, and asked for "increased coordination among US and EU regulators" (though the United States had been notably absent from important environmental agreements over the previous two years).

American troops massed on the Kuwait/Iraq border as a delegation of State Department officials joined two Dow chemical company executives in Athens to lobby the Greeks, who then held the presidency of the European Union, to oppose REACH.[38] Colin Powell himself sent out a seven-page cable to U.S. embassies in Europe, claiming that REACH "could present obstacles to trade" and cost U.S. chemical producers "tens of billions of dollars" in lost exports. The cable stated that application of the precautionary principle was "problematic"—thereby striking at the heart of the difference between the United States and European regulatory approaches toward environmental hazards. These were the kickoffs to an unprecedented international lobbying effort by the Bush administration to block REACH from being passed into law. By putting chemicals through the rigors of review, a Commerce Department paper warned, "hundreds of thousands of Americans could be thrown out of their jobs." U.S. trade representative Robert Zoellick submitted a protest to the World Trade Organization's Technical Barriers to Trade Committee, asserting that REACH amounted to a "non-tariff" obstacle to foreign exporters.[39] At the same time, the administration sent emissaries to the new EU members like Hungary, Poland, Estonia, and the Czech Republic, formerly communist countries where environmental consciousness was far less developed than it is in Western Europe, where it tried to peel off support by claiming that REACH would make it more difficult for European firms to compete against American firms in foreign markets.

The European Commission came to a different conclusion. After conducting numerous game-playing exercises with industry, and commissioning at least forty feasibility studies, the commission estimated that the cost to the global chemical industry for complying with REACH would be 2.3 billion ($2.7 billion) over eleven years. Costs for all industry, mostly for collecting toxicity data or preparing already-existing data never before released to either government or the public, were estimated to be between 2.8 billion and 5.2 billion ($3.5 billion and $6 billion). A European chemical-industry-sponsored feasibility study by the international accounting firm KPMG came to a similar conclusion: that REACH would cost $8 billion to all industries over the next eleven years—a figure that amounts to about 0.10 percent of 2005 chemical sales in Europe. The commission further calculated that the costs of REACH would be repaid many times over by its benefits—including the prevention of 4,500 occupational cancer deaths each year, and saving some $60 billion over three decades that the commission predicted would accrue to the European public, by reducing the costs of health care from ailments related to chemical exposure.[40]

By asking for substitution of particularly toxic chemicals by less toxic substances "when feasible"—and creating an independent agency to judge that feasibility—REACH aimed to take the worst substances out of circulation altogether. REACH was not a barrier to trade, the EU claimed in a submission to the World Trade Organization, because it applied equally to its own and to foreign manufacturers. It trumpeted the opportunities for "green" chemical research that would be encouraged by the first open, actually free market in chemicals—in which consumers would be given information enabling them to make the decision as to what risks they are willing to take.

An aggressive effort by the State and Commerce departments to recruit allies to oppose REACH was begun. Pleas went out from the U.S. and Australian missions in Brussels to countries like India, Malaysia, Brazil, South Africa, and Japan to develop a "coordinated outreach" strategy among "EU trading partners on REACH. Those countries are heavily reliant on exports; their products, like those of U.S. manufacturers, would be subject to Europe's new toxic screen.

Chemicals, the Commerce Department claims, account for 35 percent of the value of all footwear, 16 percent of the value in motor vehicles, and 15 percent of the value in jewelry—and that's just skimming the surface of the industries that would be affected by REACH. I sat in parliamentary hearings where I was able to identify lobbyists not only for the U.S. and European chemical industries, but representatives of "downstream" chemical users from U.S. cement, automobile, packaging, textile, and pharmaceutical companies. Also in attendance were representatives of South African mining companies, Japanese electronics firms, and the big British retail outlet Boots.

Administration officials and industry lobbyists were "knocking down the doors to get meetings with us," according to Christina Travagliati, chief legislative aid to Guido Sacconi, an Italian Socialist MEP on the Environment Committee. Sacconi played a critical role in negotiating REACH with the committee's Christian Democratic chair over three years. Travagliati told me her office was deluged with visits from U.S. State, Commerce, United States Trade Representative, and chemical-industry officials. She even received a personal letter from Colin Powell appealing to her boss to give up on REACH. "We were disappointed and astonished at the same time," she recalled. "It is not the competence of the American authorities to lobby against these regulations. We saw it as a kind of intrusion into our business. We are perfectly competent at doing this business ourselves."[41]

In July 2005, I attended a meeting in Brussels organized by the German state of North-Rhine Westphalia, center of the German chemical industry. The gathering, in a turn-of-the-century Brussels mansion now occupied by representatives of one of Europe's most powerful industrial regions, was organized for MEPs and parliamentary aides to give vent to Europe's own chemical industry's concerns about REACH. There in the outdoor garden, sipping fine German Riesling during the cocktail party beforehand, I found Michael Walls, director of the American Chemical Council, the main lobbyist for the U.S. chemical industry. Walls and other top U.S. chemical representatives were making regular forays into Brussels to express their opposition. I approached Walls to ask him questions about U.S. industry concerns; "Not talking now," he smiled, and walked away. Back in the States, I put in repeated requests for an interview, to which Walls did not respond. The closest to a comment from the American Chemical Council I received was from Tiffany Harrington, a policy analyst on regulatory issues for the trade association, who commented: "TSCA is not broken. The EPA is not broken. There is no need for an untested policy like REACH. We just have to know how to handle chemicals . . . Look at table salt," she added, "in large doses that can kill a person too."[42]

U.S. lobbying left a sour taste even among those who are the Bush administration's more natural ideological allies—notable among them Karl Heinz Florenz, the Christian Democrat from Germany who as Environment Committee chairman was responsible for developing consensus on REACH with Sacconi's Socialists. Florenz was courted by the administration, according to his aide, Peter Schmitt, and even invited to Washington in the spring of 2005 for an "exchange of views" with the State Department. Schmitt accompanied Florenz on that trip and recalled the administration's position: "Kill REACH. That was it.

There was no in-between." He said that hard-line position backfired. "What the Americans still do not understand," he said, "is that even for us Christian Democrats, the environment is a big issue."[43]

I made numerous efforts to speak with Charles Auer, who deals most directly with U.S. chemical enforcement as director of the EPA's Office of Pollution Prevention and Toxics. Auer's domain would be most directly affected by REACH; he was one of those U.S. officials who had been making regular appearances in parliamentary and commission offices to argue against it. Auer declined, through EPA intermediaries, my repeated requests for an interview through the spring and summer of 2006. Finally, in an e-mail in September, he stated simply: "Thanks for the offer but because EPA is principally a domestic agency and this topic involves legislative and regulatory matters in another jurisdiction, it is my practice not to engage on such topics with the press."[44]

The same month that Auer sent his polite rebuff, Robert Donkers was traveling across the United States addressing business associations in California, Texas, and Massachusetts to answer concerns among executives and product designers about what the new initiatives coming from that "other jurisdiction" in Europe would mean for their businesses.

U.S. lobbying amounted to a historic intrusion into European affairs. Donkers invited me to consider the reverse scenario: European officials descending on Washington to lobby against a bill being considered by the U.S. Congress. "It wouldn't be tolerated," he exclaimed. "We wouldn't last ten minutes!"

American Missionary in Brussels

In an Environment Committee hearing room at the European Parliament, I watched, one morning in the fall of 2005, as more than seven hundred amendments that had been appended to REACH were voted on in rapid succession. As each new amendment was announced by the chairman, Karl Heinz Florenz, and translators in skyboxes above relayed them in eleven different languages, the forty-six members of the committee watched for three thumbs at the front of the room. Pointing up or pointing down, the thumbs signaled recommended votes to members of the committee from the committee's three main parliamentary groups: the People's Party coalition of Christian Democrats, the Socialists, and a coalition of Greens and other leftist parties. "Down" went "mandatory substitution," a defeat for environmentalists, to be replaced by "substitution when safer alternatives are available"; "up" went more public information to be made available for "substances of very high concern." Over more than two hours, as each amendment was agreed upon or ousted, the outlines of an agreement between the Christian Democrats and Socialists took form.

From Washington, however, President Bush signaled that the struggle was far from over: He nominated a man to be the new U.S. ambassador to the European Union who was tailor-made for killing or weakening REACH before it was passed into law. C. Boyden Gray, a veteran Republican operative and an heir to the RJ Reynolds tobacco fortune, had spent a career in and out of government rewriting the rules of environmental risk to reduce oversight of business. Now he was given the chance to take that agenda overseas.

Gray began his assault on U.S. regulation when he served as a White House counsel to the Presidential Task Force on Regulatory Reform during the Reagan administration, and then as general counsel to President George H. W. Bush from 1989 to 1993. Among his primary legacies was empowering the Office of Management and Budget to begin applying cost-benefit analyses over risk-based decision making by EPA and other federal oversight agencies. After Bush Sr. lost his bid for reelection, Gray continued his deregulatory crusade from outside government.

In the 1990s, Gray was cochairman of Citizens for a Sound Economy, funded primarily by the chemical and oil industries to lobby for "pro-growth" regulatory policies. During this time he also served on the board of the Center for Risk Analysis at Harvard University—which specializes in statistical studies of comparative risk and what it calls "cost-effectiveness analysis." They weigh, for example, the risk from automobile accidents versus chemical exposure, and advocating policies that reflect the greater acute danger from the former. The center acts as an intellectual farm team for advocates of environmental deregulation, and has provided some of President George W. Bush's key regulatory-agency appointments. Among those are the center's former president, John Graham, who was appointed head of the Office of Management and Budget. In that position, Graham went on to accelerate many of the internal rule changes that Gray had advocated during his tenure in the White House under Bush Sr.

In 2002, Gray went after the other critical leg of environmental protection: the judiciary. He cofounded the Committee for Justice, which played a central role in supporting President Bush's judicial nominees, many of whom are drawn from the very industries overseen by the EPA. According to a report by the Center for Investigative Reporting, between 2001 and 2004 more than one third of President Bush's nominees—twenty-one out of fifty-nine—had a history of working as lawyers and lobbyists on behalf of the oil, gas, and energy industries.[45] The Committee for Justice works with the National Association of Manufacturers to place more corporate-friendly judges on the bench. In 2004, the group provided at least five million dollars to campaigns aimed at defeating judges deemed to have issued "antibusiness" opinions, according to the *Wall Street Journal*.[46] These efforts were part of the "tort reform" campaigns in the states being funded by Procter & Gamble and other companies. When I spoke with Ambassador Gray in September 2006, he called these the "brushfires" that remained from two decades of regulatory retrenchment. The single biggest contributor to the Committee for Justice's multimillion dollar campaign fund was the U.S. Chamber of Commerce—the industry trade association to which AmCham EU in Brussels pays yearly membership dues.

AmCham EU's managing director Susan Danger told me that she and a delegation of the group's members met with Gray in Washington and discussed REACH in the fall of 2005—two months after his nomination by President Bush, and four months before he moved from Washington to Brussels.[47] In February 2006, Gray took his agenda across the sea with all the strings of diplomatic influence at his disposal. REACH was on the top of his agenda. "In the person of C. Boyden Gray," commented Daryl Ditz, senior policy adviser to the Center for International Environmental Law (CIEL), "you have a missionary sent to Brussels to carry the gospel of American risk management."[48]

By the time Gray landed in Europe, REACH had undergone a rewrite by the European Commission, had passed its first reading in the parliament, and was awaiting review by the Council of Ministers. Nearly one thousand amendments had been voted on and consolidated, partly from that Environment Committee vote six months earlier. The act had been weakened in significant ways. Priority had been put on "high-volume chemicals"—produced in excess of ten tons a year, with diminishing data requirements as the volume declined—and broad exemptions were issued for monomers, binding agents, and plastics (which are also covered by other EU laws). But REACH still retained its historic principles: that thousands of existing chemicals would be reviewed for their toxicity; that the data from those reviews would be made public; and that responsibility for demonstrating a chemical's safety rests with the manufacturers.

Gray was born into one of the leading families in North Carolina and speaks with the genial tones of the southern aristocracy. He is an

American history buff, and when I spoke with him by phone during one of his visits back to Washington, he wanted to discuss how the tensions that surface periodically in the EU between the central authority in Brussels and the member states have their echo in the first century of the American republic, when states were testing their power against that of the federal government. "They are fighting the battle between Thomas Jefferson and Alexander Hamilton!" he exclaimed. "This is a battle we resolved over a hundred years ago." (He's right. Hamilton's view of a strong executive limiting the autonomy of the states ultimately prevailed over Jefferson's aim to give the states greater autonomy, a principle over which the United States fought a civil war. Europeans are now engaged in a similar struggle as the commission sketches out its authority over the member states through legal battles in the European Court of Justice; the desire of EU members like Austria to impose more strict standards over genetically modified organisms, for example, was ultimately trumped by Brussels' growing transnational authority).

Gray's boisterous southern charm turns vehement, though, on the subject of the Europeans' approach to regulation: "The battle they're fighting [in Europe] now was fought and won in this country in the 1980s, mostly during the Reagan administration." Gray was referring to the struggle in the United States, in which he had been a critical player, over regulatory retrenchment. "We went through this," he said. "This is the beast [in the U.S.] we have confined and tamed. . . . I am struggling to find what human lives will be saved by REACH, other than all those bureaucrats filling out new forms." REACH, he said, would "choke economic growth" and "be hell for American multinationals. . . . Our position is if we don't stop it, it will multiply like kudzu."[49]

On June 9, 2006, the U.S. embassy issued a press release stating that the United States and nine other countries—including Brazil, South Africa, Korea, India, Mexico, and Japan—objected to REACH's "hazard-based" system for assessing risks, and called for weakening its registration requirements, the regulation's *raison d'être*. It was one of Gray's first public acts as ambassador. All the U.S.-allied signatories are significant export economies, with a lot at stake in whose standards would govern their production. The complaints were the same as had been coming out of the Bush administration for three years, as if the substantial compromises by REACH's most fervent advocates had never happened.

But there was something else about that press release that was more revealing than its predictable content. One morning in my e-mail I discovered a leaked copy of the original draft, including the editorial changes made by Microsoft tracking software as the press release made its way through various readers. Thirty-seven changes were made through the one-and-a-half-page document, each one initialed and dated. Most were minor deletions and additions, grammatical corrections and the like. But deletion number 1 was quite revealing. Deleted were an address, phone number, and fax. The address was 53 Avenue Arts et Loi, B-1000, Brussels, Belgium. That's the address of AmCham EU, the major lobbying force in Europe representing U.S. industry. A date was also removed, June 8. By the time the announcement was sent out to the press on June 9, the document was tidily edited and released. Where AmCham EU's address had been now ran the imprimatur of the "United States Mission to the European Union."[50] Thanks to Microsoft—which incidentally was hit with a $357 million fine for anticompetitive behavior in Europe a month later—we were offered an extraordinary glimpse into the routine merging of U.S. government and private interests that were driving American resistance to REACH. (The leaked document would ultimately make its way into the *EU Observer*, the *Economist*-run weekly that covers the EU in Brussels which ran a bemused item headlined: "Microsoft Scuppers U.S. REACH Lobby.") When I asked Ambassador Gray about the incident, he shrugged it off, saying, simply: "They sponsored the meeting. We wrote the press release."

Three months after the AmCham EU incident, as the Environment Committee prepared for its final vote on REACH, the U.S. embassy sent out another e-mail. This one offered the United States' recommendations to committee members on how to vote— in each case, votes that would weaken REACH.[51] Rather than triggering a mass turn of the tide against REACH, however, the incidents together infuriated the Europeans and came close to igniting a diplomatic protest. One European diplomat commented, "If their only message is why we should not do anything more than they're already doing in the United States, then why should we listen? The more the United States gives the impression of mounting an attack against REACH, the less we listen. . . . We are not going to ask the United States for permission. If we were to listen to the United States, how would we explain to European citizens where the two hundred chemicals in their bodies came from? What are they doing to them? This is the same not just for Europeans, but for Americans and for every country in the world."[52]

When I spoke with Ambassador Gray, he seemed surprised that U.S. lobbying did not seem to be working. He expressed a sense of fatalism that somehow history's tide was indeed turning. Despite his best efforts, there was not much more that could be done about the Europeans' "goofy" initiative. "Our multinationals," he said, "will have to go with the toughest standards. We are surrounded. Our system is getting squeezed out. If we get surrounded, after awhile nobody pays attention to you anymore. Its like musical chairs: who's the last one standing?"

The final overthrow of TSCA, and America's leading role in establishing the parameters of chemical regulation, was struck on December 13, 2006, in Strasbourg during a tumultuous meeting of the European Parliament. On that day, the parliament voted to make REACH the law, effective June 1, 2007. Manufacturers have eleven years from that date to prepare for what amounts to a scientific cataloguing of the risks of the underlying chemical makeup of the global economy—a rendering of the periodic table suggesting not only the immense possibilities for new chemical combinations, but also the risks that come along with those innovations.[53]

From its inception to final passage, REACH had gone through many changes. Environmentalists in Europe thought they had been sold out by some of the compromises, including the diminishing data requirements for substances produced in amounts of ten tons a year or less, and the removal of mandatory substitution requirements for hazardous substances in favor of obligating producers to submit plans for developing substitutes within six years of submitting a registration request. Industry was also unhappy; they had had to agree to the basic principle that it was the producers' responsibility to demonstrate the safety of their products. As for Eleonora Bruno, who followed the developments closely from her home in Bari, Italy, she wrote me to say: "I know it's not perfect, there are some loopholes, but it's an important step: the politicians have taken note that there's a huge problem, and are trying to solve it. I prefer an imperfect law in comparison to nothing at all. . . . In the context of European research this database will help generate knowledge and innovations. Ultimately, it will also help to improve basic understanding of chemical structures and their effects."[54]

By the end of 2008, the first sets of risk data are to be submitted as part of the "preregistration" for all chemicals on the market. A list of "substances of very high concern"—carcinogens, mutagens, and reproductive toxins that are considered bio-accumulative—is being compiled. These will be the first to be removed from the market unless producers can demonstrate that they can be "adequately controlled." Donkers told me that this list could amount to as many as fifteen hundred substances, including those nonstick chemicals and flame retardants that were found in the blood of Eleonora Bruno and her bio-monitored counterparts in America.

Malcolm Woolf, whom I spoke with when he was chief legislative counsel to the then-Democratic minority on the Senate Environment and Public Works Committee (and is now a policy adviser on natural resources to the National Governors Association), told me that the European's push toward tighter safety regulations signals the end of TSCA. He predicted it would be just a matter of several years before TSCA would be amended in the United States, and its regulatory standards adjusted upward to match those of Europe. The irony is that much of the pressure to do so, he said, will likely come from industry, which has long resisted the reforms embodied in REACH. Now, he said, "They will want to harmonize with Europe to prevent their competitors, who don't export there, from gaining competitive advantage."[55] (It appears those reform efforts are gathering steam under the new Obama administration.)

Once it was TSCA that fundamentally changed the market. A quarter-century later, a new market shift is upon us. "Companies around the world have been buying chemicals based on function, price, and performance," commented Mike Wilson, the environmental health scientist at University of California–Berkeley. "Hazard has not been a part of that picture. REACH is going to start driving that information to downstream users, who will for the first time be able to make comparisons between one substance and another. So, the question of hazard will start to be considered on an equal footing with those other criteria in making choices. Say you're a manufacturer and you're looking around the world to buy the chemicals you need. You want to sell in Europe, as well as wherever else you can sell. Whose chemicals are you going to buy? The European ones that have undergone a screen for their toxicity, or the American ones that have not?" Wilson paused. "Consumers will be faced with the same types of choices."[56]

The vote for REACH was heard around the world. Most poignantly, it was heard in the so-called emerging economies, which the *Economist* pegs as the future economic engines of the twenty-first century, with growth rates exceeding those of both Europe and the United States. They, too, will be faced with similar choices. Will China, India, Brazil, and other rapidly developing countries look to Brussels or to Washington for leadership on how to prepare for the environmental pressures that have been accompanying their high-speed growth? From whom will they buy the products, and look to for ideas, that might offer some sustainable solutions to their own looming environmental crises?

8

Transpacific Drift:
China and the Next Big Thing

The European Commission took REACH on the road. To make it work, the manufacturing powerhouses of the new global economy had to be on board.

Within days of REACH passing in the parliament, emissaries were sent from Europe to inform manufacturers around the world of the new toxic screening imperatives it demands. The European Commission knows," said Stacy Vandeveer at Brown University, "that there is a global competition over who's setting the global standards."[1] The cold war drove an arms race between ideological adversaries; today it is economic competition among the world's superpowers that marks the new century, and data gaps between friends have replaced missile gaps between enemies. The United States accounts for about 20 percent of all so-called REACH exports; 38 percent come from developing countries—foremost among them South Africa, China, Chile, Brazil, and India, in order of magnitude according to a Tufts University study of REACH's impacts on trade comissioned by the EU's Directorate General for External Policies.[2] These and other emerging economies, according to the Organization for Economic Cooperation and Development, will be responsible for increasing percentages of the world's chemicals, minerals, and manufactured goods over the coming decades. This is where the action moves to in establishing new guideposts for environmental protection.

Nowhere have the implications of this dynamic become clearer than in China—the room from which comes the elephant of the global economy. The unprecedented 9 percent a year that China's economy has been growing since 2001, the 25 percent of the world's steel it consumes, the 10 percent of the world's electricity, the 30 percent of its coal, the coal-fired power plant it is building every week, entices and haunts Europeans and Americans alike. McKinsey & Company predicts that at the current rate of growth, one quarter of the world's total factory output will come from China by 2025.[3] In this sense, Americans and Europeans have been united in their lust for China's vast markets and fear of its potentially devastating competitiveness. An ever-greater percentage of the world's shoes, computer parts, toys, cosmetics, textiles, television sets, and automobiles will come from Chinese factories.

But there is another figure buried in these astounding signs of China's roaring new presence in the international economy. Sixty percent of China's exports are produced by affiliates of multinational corporations.[4] It is not Chinese companies alone that are consuming resources at a voracious clip and competing against their American or European counterparts, but multinational firms competing among each other, all manufacturing in China or wherever else in the world they can exact the best price. (In fact, that Tufts University study found that most of the REACH exports manufactured in developing countries in Africa, the Caribbean, and the Pacific also come from multinational firms, of European as well as African, Asian, and North American origin.) Branding (the Nike swoosh or the Hasbro decal) is what happens after a product leaves a Chinese factory and is shipped to its overseas buyer. A key question, then, over the coming decades is: According to whose product-safety standards will those factories produce? Here, as in the other emerging economies, is where the power plays of the twenty-first century are unfolding, where Europe and America are maneuvering for influence in the territory of the world's other great economic powers. And who will have the technology to match those standards?

A desire to avoid the shortsightedness of the West is growing as the environmental consequences of China's rapid development hit home. As many as 700,000 deaths a year in China are attributable to air pollution, according to the World Bank.[5] The head of the country's State Environmental Protection Administration (SEPA) estimates the economic losses from pollution and environmental damage amount to the equivalent of ten percent of the GDP every year.[6] Nor is China's immense environmental degradation confined within its borders; pollution from Chinese industry sends soot east into Korea, north into Japan, and east across the Pacific to California. The gases it sends into the atmosphere are the most significant contributor to global warming (though the U.S. is a close second).

"China is undergoing a wholesale reassessment of its environmental policies," Tseming Yang, a professor at Vermont Law School, told me shortly after returning from a spring semester in 2006 teaching environmental law at Beijing University.[7] Yang has been traveling to China regularly to help with educating a new generation in the legal principles of environmental protection. He is one of a growing number of scholars, technicians, and non-governmental organizations from America and Europe who have been flooding China with expertise about how to address the country's array of massive environmental challenges. China's budding citizens' movement is also finding ways to use the nascent system of environmental laws to provide accountability and enforcement, though often against harsh resistance from local government authorities.

China is now looking inward for more sustainable development strategies and outward for new ideas on which to base its young and evolving system of environmental protections and oversight. In the process, China has become a playing field for international influence driven partly by the desire to address the country's huge contribution to climate change, and partly for positioning in anticipation of the economic bonanza that is already beginning to come from the development of alternative, renewable energy technologies. On both counts, the United States is falling behind the European Union. Beijing already sees that many new rules governing China's economic future are being written in Brussels and not Washington. As Ambassador Gray put it to me: "The Europeans have been selling the Chinese very hard. The United States has to start counter-selling."[8] It may be too late.

March 2007 hit like a power surge for Panasonic, Intel, Sony, and the rest of the global electronics industry. Eight months after RoHS, the EU's directive banning all hazardous chemicals and minerals in electronic devices, the Chinese equivalent came into force: the "Administration on the Control of Pollution Caused by Electronic Information Products" sent a signal that China would no longer allow itself to be the world's dumping ground for hazardous products.[9]

As a Basel Action Network investigation showed, at least 50 percent of the e-waste that is collected for recycling in the United States is shipped to scrap yeards in developing countries like Taiwan, the Philippines, Nigeria, and China.[10] In Chinese port cities and rural provinces like Taizhou and Guangdong, the rotting heaps of computers, appliances, VCRs, telephones, and other electronic trash break down, and as they decay the pent-up toxins that once helped make them hum with efficiency or sparkle with light or memorize millions of words, leak through the soil, into the water supply, and eventually the bloodstreams of nearby inhabitants. In Chinese cities that have become the center of the e-waste trade, carcinogens have been found in reservoirs, and brain-damaging levels of lead have been found in children.

China's new standards are drawn directly from European Union regulations, and target the same six toxic chemicals and minerals as the European RoHS directive: lead, mercury, cadmium, hexavalent chromium, and PBDE flame retardants. The derisive moniker "made in China"—long associated with dismal safety protections— is being turned inside-out as U.S. electronics companies must now demonstrate the safety of their products for Chinese consumers.

There are some distinctions between the Chinese and European controls: the Europeans rely on companies to declare their RoHS compliance, and then penalize violators; the Chinese require that testing be conducted in Chinese labs before manufacturers are given a certificate of compliance. Maximum acceptable levels for the six substances are fixed at the same level in China and in Europe, ranging from 0.1 percent to 0.01 percent of each substance, depending on where in the product they are found, and their potential for migrating out. For products exceeding the maximum, China has devised a potent innovation, labeling. Manufacturers are obliged to inform consumers how long their product may be used before the expiration of its "environmental-protection use period," known as EPUP—a term coined by the Ministry of Information Industries to describe when toxics start to present a health or environmental hazard. The number is printed in an orange circle in a label on every one of the hundreds of products covered by the new law; an explanation of why must be included in the owner's manual. So, for example, cathode-ray television sets are given a number 7, and cell phones a 20, for the number of years they can be used before springing a toxic leak.

In its original version in 2005, the Chinese used the phrase "environmentally safe" to define the acceptable use period. But lobbyists from the American Electronics Association, which opened up a lobbying arm in Beijing that year, succeeded in convincing the Chinese to switch to the less loaded EPUP. "Having the word 'safe' implies a condition that could be its opposite," an electronics industry consultant told me.[11] In a second stage, starting in March 2009, none of those substances will be permitted in electronic information products any longer, putting the country in alignment with the European Union. (Like the EU, the Chinese will issue exemptions if companies can demonstrate there are no viable alternatives.)

Europe's determination to cleanse some of the most pervasive products of their toxins kicked off a domino effect from Brussels to Beijing and beyond. "Europe," says Kirschner, "is now the arbiter of materials used to build everything from appliances in the kitchen to the car in your garage."[12] Over the course of 2006, Taiwan, Thailand, Korea, Japan, Australia, Canada, and Mexico introduced their own versions of RoHS, with the same substances first identified by the European Union targeted for removal, either directly through bans or severe content restrictions, or indirectly through labeling. An industry that American inventors played a large role in creating is discovering it must be reshaped because their foreign buyers (and in China's case, manufacturers) are asserting more sustainable and less environmentally destructive means of production.

China is the world's largest manufacturer of electronics; in 2005, it sent $85 billion in electronic exports to the U.S. and $33 billion to the EU.[13] What China's markets require, its manufacturers—or, more precisely, the outsourced manufacturers for foreign companies—produce.

Just as Kirschner works with American firms on adapting to the European RoHS, he works with China-based firms in Hong Kong and Shanghai that want to retain access to the 1.3 billion strong Chinese domestic market, whose appetite for electronics is growing. For many mainstream producers—Panasonic, Sony, Apple, Dell, Hewlett Packard, and others—complying with the restrictions in China or Europe or Japan (home to several of the major multinational producers) is now part of the business plan. The bulk of Kirschner's business is now consulting on the environmental standards of foreign countries, because in the United States there are no chemical controls over the production of electronics. "What the Europeans say stays, stays," he said. "And what they say goes, goes. The [U.S.] federal government is nowhere to be found."

China's restrictions on hazardous substances apply only to its domestic market; exports are exempted. Thus, a new category of goods may be manufactured in China but not sold to its citizens. To whose citizens may those products be sold? To Americans. And to citizens in countries with even fewer environmental protections in Africa, Asia, and Latin America. Those producers who opt not to export to Europe, or China, or any of the other countries adapting the RoHS guidelines as their own—what Rick Goss of the Electrical Industries Alliance calls the no-name "white-box manufacturers"—go where the controls are weakest.

Dominoes used to be the favored game of the cold war, as countries tipped one way or another to the American or Soviet spheres of influence. Now, though, the domino effect is no longer an ideological contest, but is triggered by the muscle of the market. Just like Europe's RoHS directive, it did not take long for news of REACH to travel into China, where the State Environmental Protection Agency (SEPA) has been seeking new ways of controlling the dangers from hazardous chemicals.

Just a decade ago, the new ideas being assessed in China were embodied in a different law. In 1996, the Environmental Protection Agency's then-administrator for toxics Lynn Goldman was sent to Beijing to meet her freshly appointed counterparts at SEPA.: "I've never forgotten that trip," she recalled. "They had a brand new chemical agency. They had just translated TSCA into Chinese, and presented it to me as a gift." Goldman still has that Mandarin language version of the Toxic Substances Control Act on her bookshelf at Johns Hopkins.[14] Today, though, the translated law sitting on officials' desks in Beijing is not TSCA, but REACH.

In recent years, the four-star Maison du Dragon hotel in central Brussels has been a redoubt for Chinese delegations visiting with European diplomats, scientists, and officials with the Environment and Energy directorates. Qi Ye, director of the Institute of Public Policy at Tsinghua University in Beijing, told me in the spring of 2006 that he has been leading regular trips for government officials to Brussels to "consult with the Europeans on many things: chemicals, climate change, environmental governance."[15] China sells $19 billion a year worth of chemicals to the European Union, and billions more worth of chemical-containing consumer products. All would be subject to REACH.

One week after REACH's final passage in December 2006 in Strasbourg, Zhang Xiangchen, director of the World Trade Organization Affairs Department of the Ministry of Commerce, announced in comments reported by the Xinhua News Service that the Chinese government would immediately begin consulting with local industries to help them comply with the new European directive. The government, Zhang said, would assist chemical companies in developing their "risk controlling ability."[16] European consultants would also begin working with Chinese industry and government officials, aiding with the data collection and toxicity testing they would need in order to ensure continued access to European markets. By the end of 2008, the Chinese had begun the process of submitting toxicity data reports for the high-volume chemicals—those sold in quantities of more than one hundred tons a year—it exports to Europe. All other exporters, as well as domestic European producers, will have to do the same. The European approach to determining risk—not America's—was being implanted into Chinese policy making.

Why would the Europeans be working to aid their competitors in China, with whom both Europe and America share a significant trade deficit? I asked this question of the one other European diplomat whose post is akin to Robert Donkers' in Washington: Magnus Gislev, a Swede, who was appointed the EU's environment counselor in China in early 2006. Gislev arrived in China, he told me in a telephone interview from the EU's mission in Beijing, shortly after a disastrous chemical explosion that released highly toxic benzene into the Songhua River and poisoned the water supply for some 4 million inhabitants in the northern city of Harbin. He has a mandate similar to that of Donkers' in the United States—though of course with a far more daunting set of environmental challenges—including air and water pollution, energy efficiency, and protection from hazardous chemicals. About REACH, Gislev commented, "We are looking down the supply chain. A lot of our downstream users do business with the Chinese."[17] In other words, the makers of all those Chinese consumer items—the toys, the textiles, the electronics, the shoes, the plastic wrap, and everything else that uses chemicals made by Chinese firms—ultimately end up in the hands of Europeans. To protect its population, Europe is working backward toward the source of potential future chemical contamination. In this way, Europe has a vested interest in bringing Chinese industry into compliance with REACH, as it does with India, Brazil, and all the other sources of its outsourced manufacturing.

"There are challenges that come with establishing a new standard for the world," Nicolas Thery at the EU Trade Directorate had told me back in Brussels. "The question is: What kind of international consequences will these new standards have? Do we impose on developing countries this same environmental approach? Or do we permit 'dirty' industries to move elsewhere from Europe, and thus get a division between environmental havens and lands of waste?" The EU made a decision, Thery said, to work with its developing country partners in the global economy to assist them in meeting Europe's more rigorous requirements. "If you export your problems abroad," he added, "then that's a problem."[18] The EU's international promotion of its environmental initiatives, though, is not being driven purely by beneficence: standing alone in the world with higher standards could in the long run put its businesses at a competitive disadvantage.

Orville Schell, who has written eleven books and numerous dispatches for the *New Yorker* on China, and is now head of U.S.-China programs for the Asia Society, cautioned that laws on the books in China do not necessarily mean enforcement. "China," he said, "is notorious for having laws in Beijing that are completely unenforced at the provincial level. In Beijing they may be getting more enlightened, but state and local governments have been quite resistant to any environmental reforms."[19] Indeed, in a system not known for its public accountability, the means of holding local government authorities to the letter of laws written in Beijing are minimal. The State Environmental Protection Administration has just three hundred employees—compared to, say, the EPA, which has some thirty thousand. As Schell suggests, many initiatives from Beijing are flouted in the Chinese provinces. The difference, however, with the environmental standards now flowing from Europe is that enforcement does not come necessarily from Beijing, or from within China, but from the market dynamics of international trade. It is, in essence, the European Union that will enforce standards for Chinese industry by ensuring the safety of products destined for its markets. The lucrative European market is both carrot and stick. It may take some years before the Chinese impose reliable enforcement on a national level. But by establishing strict import standards, the Europeans have set powerful incentives into motion for China's own domestic manufacturers.

C. S. Kiang, the dean of environmental studies at Peking University in Beijing—who was brought to the University of California–Berkeley Graduate School of Journalism by Orville Schell, the former dean, for several weeks of guest teaching—told me that the effect of initiatives like REACH and RoHS in China will be to open to greater public scrutiny a system that has been traditionally secretive and unaccountable. This may end up being the most profound impact of the changes initiated in Brussels. "REACH pushes us to move into a knowledge-based system," Kiang said. "For the first time, this sector will have to be governed by the rule of law— of accountability and transparency. This is a very significant change for China."[20]

It is the carrot-stick dynamic, Gislev predicts, that will provide a powerful impetus toward compliance. The EU, not the United States, is China's biggest market. "Most export-oriented economies," Gislev said, "tend to go with the standards of their biggest markets." Gislev estimates that within five years the Chinese will have a substantial set of new laws that will reflect the basic principles embedded in REACH. When that does happen, the EPA will have little power under the current version of TSCA to prevent the importation of substances into the United States from China that the new European Chemicals Agency refuses to "authorize" for sale in Europe.

That's already happening. China exports five hundred million dollars a year worth of processed wood to the United States that's been treated with formaldehyde, a binder in plywood and other home- and office-construction materials. Formaldehyde is a "known carcinogen," according to the International Agency for Research on Cancer, and a contributor to asthma in young children and respiratory problems in adults, according to the Harvard School of Public Health and other research centers. In the spring of 2006 a timber company in Oregon, Columbia Forest Products, conducted tests of imported Chinese birch planks that it had purchased at a Home

Depot (such tests are not done by the U.S. government, thus our primary information on such matters comes from the private sector or NGOs). The company discovered levels of formaldehyde far in excess of permissible levels in either Europe or Japan, China's largest two markets for wood products after the U.S. The wood contained 3.0 parts per million of formaldehyde—thirty times the acceptable European levels of 0.1 parts per million. The Chinese wood industry, according to Michael Wolfe, a partner in the consulting firm, Hooper-Wolfe, which specializes in sustainable manufacturing, "has the capacity to produce high-end products without formaldehyde, like those demanded by Europe and Japan, and very low-end products that contain it. By having no standards in the United States, the Chinese are dumping products here which they can't unload in Europe or Japan."[21]

Nor, in the long run, are the Chinese seemingly content with emulating Europe's or any other nation's standards. China's admission to the World Trade Organization in 2001 spurred debate inside the highest ranks of the government over which country would establish the standards by which major producers in the global economy must abide. The Chinese concluded that, over time, it would be their own. The scholarly journal *Asia Policy* published a paper coauthored by Chaoyi Zhao, a research fellow at the China National Institute of Standardization, a division within China's government standard-setting apparatus, and John M. Graham, a Next Generation Fellow at the National Bureau of Asian Research, a U.S. think tank affiliated with Tsinghua University. The two men wrote of the largely unrecognized competitive power that lies behind the setting of standards—whether they be standards governing technology, safety, and financial management, or those governing environmental protection. China's strategy, the authors concluded, "is to move the country from being a net importer of international standards to that of producer of standards for international consumption."[22] China's enormous economic heft suggests that, over decades, this is not an implausible dream. In the realm of chemicals, when and if this change begins to happen, the country will be starting from a baseline now being set by the European Union.

China's vast economic and ecological footprint is not only reshaping the global economy, it is reshaping the global climate. Year after year of double-digit growth requires vast and increasing supplies of energy to keep pace. China is second only to the United States as a greenhouse gas emitter. At the end of 2006, it released its first-ever report on the effects of climate change. The China Meteorological Administration predicted that the average temperature in China would rise by 1.3 to 2.1 degrees Celsius by 2020, and by 2.3 to 3.3 degrees Celsius by 2050. It forecast increasingly violent weather patterns that could lead to declining crop yields of as much as one third by the end of the century.

The Chinese Politburo has committed to doubling its capacity for renewable energy to 16% of national consumption by 2020, an extraordinarily ambitious goal given the Politburo's simultaneous ambition to quadruple the country's gross domestic product by that same year. The different approaches between Europe and America, in helping China meet the greatest environmental challenge of our time, were highlighted at a three-day strategic economic dialogue between top U.S. and Chinese officials during the height of the Christmas season in 2006. Attending the summit on behalf of the United States were EPA administrator Stephen Johnson, Treasury Secretary Henry Paulson, Energy Secretary Samuel Bodman, and Labor Secretary Elaine Chau. Meetings took place with the cabinet members' Chinese counterparts. REACH had passed two days earlier; China RoHS would be coming online three months later. If there were to be any environmental component to U.S. interactions with China, these would be the individuals to make them happen. But U.S. efforts are hamstrung by cold war rules that prohibit the U.S. Agency for International Development from providing any assistance to China, and by a U.S. foreign policy that is focused primarily on encouraging U.S. private businesses to strike deals with their Chinese counterparts. There was little to suggest that the Bush administration's lack of enthusiasm for environmental principles in the United States would be much different in China.

The summit concluded with a joint statement at the Great Hall of the People in Beijing, celebrating an "understanding" on both sides to encourage Chinese consumers to spend more and save less, and Americans to save more and spend less to decrease the U.S.-China trade deficit. Environmental Protection Agency administrator Stephen Johnson announced talks with Chinese officials to develop an emissions-trading market in sulfur-dioxide emissions, a market-driven strategy that has been highly successful in reducing acid rain in North America but has had little effect on greenhouse gases. Energy Secretary Bodman trumpeted a commitment by China to participate in a Department of Energy project, FutureGen, to develop a low emissions power plant by 2012 using coal gasification and carbon sequestration technology (by 2008, that project had been largely abandoned by the Bush administration). He also signed a memorandum of understanding with China's national development and reform minister, Ma Kai, to facilitate the $5.3 billion purchase of four nuclear reactors from Westinghouse. As for alternative energy, the DoE's National Renewable Energies Lab provides $100,00 to $200,000 a year worth of assistance to China, according to NREL spokesman Gary Schmitz.[23] Otherwise, the United States' primary pledge for advancing greater energy efficiency comes not in China, but at the Asia Pacific Partnership for Clean Development and Climate, a regional alliance the United States and Australia created as an alternative to Kyoto. At the group's inaugural summit in Australia in January 2006, Bodman promised $52 million to "promote clean energy technologies" in the Asia-Pacific region. One year later that money had still not been appropriated by Congress.

"The United States is not going in [to China] and saying: 'There are limited resources in the world,'" commented Jeffrey Logan, China program officer for the World Resources Institute, an environmental think tank in Washington, D.C. Logan was formerly the China program officer at the International Energy Agency, which was formed after the oil crisis of the 1970s to coordinate global energy strategies. He has been watching China's effort to balance its energy consumption with its roaring growth for more than a decade. "The United States is not saying, 'We're facing a potential crisis that you are a critical part of. How can we work together?' This has never happened. We don't have a leadership that has allowed that to happen. The United States goes in and lectures China with a lot of pomp and not much else."[24]

At the summit's concluding news conference in Beijing, Energy Secretary Bodman implored the Chinese to reduce their energy use, then was flummoxed by a simple question from a Chinese journalist. "Has the U.S. government," she asked, "ever thought of encouraging Americans to use smaller cars, for example, to save energy?"

Bodman paused. There was silence from the podium; you could hear it on the broadcast of the press conference by the public radio program "The World." The seconds ticked by like the distance Bodman had traveled. "Hmmm," he finally answered, "Yes, that's an issue."[25] The next question came, and he did not elaborate. One answer that he might have given, though highly unlikely, is that most of those American cars would never be allowed inside China because they will not meet Chinese emissions standards. When China's fuel-economy requirements take full effect in 2008, they will be five miles per gallon higher than the 27.5 miles per gallon allowed in the United States, which would thus prevent fuel-inefficient SUVs and many other American cars from being imported into China. Those Chinese standards are similar to those originated in the European Union. The Chinese have their own booming car business, so it is unlikely they would ever want to import any of ours in any case, but the alignment of European and Chinese emission regulations is a telling detail in the larger picture of how, in the struggle for influence in the great green playing field of China, the United States is being outpaced by the European Union.

"Most people assume that the United States government is playing a big role in this area," commented Mark Levine, who travels to China regularly as head of the Lawrence Berkeley Laboratory's Environmental Energy Technologies Division. Levine and a team from the laboratory's China Energy Project work directly with China's ministry of energy on technological innovations to increase efficiency. "But the Europeans are doing much better than the United States. The EU is offering discount wind generators. Canadians are offering energy-efficiency technology to China. The Swedes have a joint renewable-energy program to increase energy efficiency. . . . Other than removing the restrictions on trade in nuclear technology, there is very little that the U.S. government has brought to the table."[26]

Three weeks after Energy Secretary Bodman implored individual Chinese to reduce their energy use—and was uncertain as to whether Americans would do the same—the European Union's top diplomat, External Relations Commissioner Benita Ferrero-Waldner, announced at a summit with Chinese foreign minister Li Zhaoxing in Beijing, that the fight against global warming would henceforth be a "centerpiece" of EU foreign policy. The EU's fifteen core members, which signed the Kyoto Protocol in 1997, committed to reducing their emissions by 8 percent by 2012; new members committed to reductions of 6 to 8 percent (excluding Cyprus and Malta, which have no reduction targets).[27] Now the EU was placing this effort at the heart of European diplomacy. "There are some ideological differences between the approach of the Bush administration and that of the European Union [on climate change]," the EU's

representative Magnus Gislev explained. "The Bush administration
is betting that private business will take things in the right direction.
We believe, of course, in the role of the private sector. But they also
need strong political signals."

This sentiment was echoed by C. S. Kiang, who works closely
with Chinese environment and energy officials from his post at
Peking University. "Europe," said Kiang, "has been very aggressive in
promoting energy and environmental policies in China. The United
States has not been paying enough attention. From a business point
of view, sure, they are there. But you need a government policy,
that's missing."

European policies translate into money: $13 million (10 mil-
lion) for a feasibility study of a clean coal, carbon-sequestration
project, with technology provided by the EU; $35 million (30 mil-
lion) for aid to big industries, like cement and aluminum, for
increasing energy efficiency; and $500 million (430 million) pro-
vided by member states—Germany, the Netherlands, and Sweden
are the biggest contributors—to sixty-five different projects aimed at
increasing energy efficiency and the use of renewable energy
sources.[28] Among those sources is wind energy, which has seen a one-
hundred-fold increase in capacity since 1990. Most of the wind technology used in China, according to Yingling Liu, director of the
China Watch project—an alliance between the Washington-based
Worldwatch and the Beijing-based Global Environmental
Institute—comes from Danish, Spanish, and Dutch companies.[29]
Those three countries subsidized early development of the technology in the late eighties and nineties, and are now reaping the
profits from those public investments.

In his book, *Taming American Power: The Global Response to U.S.
Primacy*, Harvard professor Stephen Walt explored the roots of rising
resistance to U.S. leadership around the world. Walt suggests that

U.S. influence will continue to wane as long as the United States pursues policies that are perceived as being primarily motivated by self-interest.[30] But even those expressions of self-interest are starting to look shortsighted, as what at first glance looks like a natural protection of American prerogatives begins to look more like stubborn resistance to change that is happening, anyway, all over the world. U.S. economic influence is quietly fading as its political and corporate leaders fall out of step with the forces of global integration that they once avidly pressed upon the world.

U.S. environmental policies are not sparking innovation; they are fighting it. The last big piece of U.S. environmental legislation was the Clean Air Act of 1990, and it was emulated by Europe and Japan. The U.S.-devised cap-and-trade system, launched by President George H. W. Bush in 1988, was a successful American innovation on capital markets that was emulated globally and reduced the sulfur-dioxide emissions that contribute to acid rain. Now that system is being emulated on a grander scale, in the carbon-credit trading markets used by the signatories of Kyoto, to channel billions of dollars into renewable energy. The United States refuses to participate in these markets.

The Bush administration's refusal to sign the Kyoto accord is shifting business opportunities from U.S. to European innovators. Qi Ye of Tsinghua University told me he has been traveling often to London and Frankfurt to drum up investment opportunities in the carbon-offset markets there, apparently to great effect. Billions in European investments are being steered into China at those exchanges, where companies based in the Kyoto signatory countries buy and sell pollution credits, in order to meet the goals of reducing overall greenhouse gas emissions by an average of 5.2 percent below 1990 levels by 2012. European or other firms may "invest" in renewable energy programs, known in the market as clean-development mechanisms, or CDMs, in China or elsewhere in order to offset their own volume of greenhouse gas emissions. The World Bank estimates that the market in CDMs was close to $30 billion in 2006, and that sixty percent of those investments went to China.[31] Those investments were in renewable energy like wind and solar power, energy-efficiency technologies, and updating old factories to eliminate emissions like hydrofluorocarbons, which contribute to erosion of the ozone layer. The market has become so lucrative for the Chinese that the country opened its own carbon exchange in Shanghai in 2008. "China is facing a choice to either go one way on its environmental path or another," commented Yingling Liu, with the World Resources Institute's China Watch project. "The choices are now being made....[and] the United States has a lot of catching up to do with the EU in China."

Not only in China. Lynn Goldman, formerly of the EPA, sees long-term implications in the erosion of environmental credibility as other developing countries powered by their growing role in a global economy become market forces in their own right. "There will be an edge to this shift globally," she said. "For developing countries, the customers of chemical manufacturers and products, trust in the safety of those products is going to become more important. And the Europeans will have that trust."

While the United States retreats, the EU's tougher approach to environmental protection is rippling into the supply chains of the global economy. "The ground is changing," commented Daryl Ditz of the Center for International Environmental Law, which works globally on behalf of environmental reform. "It's happening through all these micro-decisions made by companies in countries most Americans don't pay attention to."[32] At the same time, new axis of power are emerging, independent of any of the superpowers. As I researched this book, a major trade deal was struck between India, Brazil, and South Africa that sent billions of dollars in commerce into motion across the hemispheres that detours the EU, U.S., and China.

In response to such emerging shifts in the gravitational pull of the global economy, the Europeans added a third to their duo of environmental counselors in Washington and Beijing. The new post is in that other rising powerhouse, India, and the mandate is the same: climate change, chemicals and more sustainable economics. The man appointed to head that effort is Robert Donkers, who in September 2007 moved from Washington to the Indian Capital of New Delhi.

9

The New Diplomats: Power & Pitfalls

Stacy Vandeveer at Brown University has seen a disconcerting change over the past several years in his graduate students: they don't believe him when he describes the groundbreaking role once played by the United States. "My students," he told me ruefully, "have no memory of U.S. environmental leadership. When I talk about how the United States was a pioneer of global environmental standards, they look stunned, like I'm some crazy apologist for the U.S. government."[1]

Presumably, Vandeveer's students, mostly twenty-somethings studying international affairs, will themselves emerge as leaders in the coming decades. Those who do will inherit an America with far less international influence than when they were born. They will be facing seminal questions of economic power: Who writes the rules? Where are the new spheres of influence in a world of so many cross-currents that even the idea of a single hegemonic power—whether European, American, or even Chinese—seems an outmoded concept of the previous century? The limits of American hard power have been on display for all to see in the quagmire of Iraq and the

Middle East; the allure once offered by American soft power—that mix of economic might and moral persuasion—has been shredded by six years of bellicose international relations. A BBC poll conducted at the end of 2006 in eighteen emerged and emerging powers like Spain, Argentina, South Africa, and Malaysia, found that just 29 percent thought U.S. influence had a "positive effect," down from 40 percent in 2004.[2]

The European Union is consolidating its influence just as U.S. influence ebbs. That "Unidentified Political Object," as former European Commission president Jacques Delors dubbed the EU, is now being seen as a model for greater political and economic integration by transnational networks like the African Union and Mercosur, the Latin American trading association. The EU and its member states are now the world's single largest supplier of foreign aid, introducing elements of environmental sustainability to economic-development strategies that were once the global purview of the United States. Despite U.S. opposition, international initiatives—among them Kyoto, the Land Mine Treaty, the International Criminal Court, the Basel Convention on Hazardous Wastes and the POPS treaty—have been moving ahead, all of them with leadership provided by the European Union. Snubbed by the Bush and in some instances the Clinton administrations, these and other environmental and human-rights initiatives have gained international legitimacy without American participation.

A question surfaces frequently in European, and occasionally American, newspapers: What is "Europe"? Is there a central idea that unifies Europe beyond the happenstance of geography and a common, often bloody, history? This question may or may not be answerable. Let's leave it to the Europeans. But as a political body, one thing is clear: "Europe" is as boisterous and disputatious and self-interested a political organism as the United States. Europe has had its share of lobbying scandals, including several instances in which industry representatives were discovered to be working improperly as "advisers" to high officials inside the European Commission.[3] Nor is the EU itself always a bucolic example of transnational cooperation; differences rage, one of them being resistance among Europeans across the political spectrum to the aggressive efforts in Brussels to harmonize environmental, financial, and other rules across a vast continent. Many in the European environmental community have been disappointed that Europe's reforms have not gone far enough; its environmental initiatives are still very much in flux.[4] In other words, Europe is like any other democracy. The argument between competitiveness and environmental protection is as alive in Brussels as it is in the United States. As Robert Donkers put it to me: "I can assure you we have no interest in driving European industry out of business."[5]

Indeed, the public struggle over these tensions is what makes the challenge presented by the EU far more interesting and provocative for the United States. The Europeans are raising the environmental bar in an economic and social context that is comparable in size and complexity to that of the United States. Their environmental strategies are not utopian, as is often portrayed in the United States; they do not arise out of some fuzzy sentimental attachment to nature. Rather, Europe is looking at the future—at the rising costs to public-health of chemical exposure; of the costs to society of waste disposal; of the ecological and political implications of addiction to oil; and of the potent impacts of excessive energy consumption, which it has led the world in fighting as a way to head off the massive ecological disruption and expense it fears will result from global warming. This is not utopian; it's more like *realpolitik* for the twenty-first century. And it is helping usher in a convergence of "green" and "economy"—two principles too often counterposed against one another in the belief that one cannot sustain the other—that is perhaps one of the most notable paradigm shifts of our era. How something is produced and with what materials is becoming a potent issue in the marketplace.

Europe is confronting industries worth hundreds of billions of dollars, representing tens of millions of jobs to its citizens, and testing the waters over whether more environmentally cognizant modes of production exact a significant economic price. The result has not been catastrophe, as predicted by European and American industry. In 2006, according to the *Wall Street Journal*, the EU's twelve-member Eurozone—the historic core of the EU (other than Britain) that uses the euro as its currency—showed a 2.7 percent growth rate, outpacing the United States, where that same year the economy grew 2.2 percent.[6] What the European approach offers, for the first time, is an ability to compare the choices taken on environmental questions of our time with comparable economic and political con-siderations at stake. What happens in Europe gives Americans a chance to weigh what might be possible in their own country.

This phenomenon is being triggered, unexpectedly enough, by the mechanisms of free trade. Globalization unleashed new sources of power with centripetal force. From Europe to emerging economies like China, Brazil, and India, trade flows are shifting and new forms of leverage emerging that the architects of a harmonized global economy never anticipated. During the cold war, power lay in the finger that held the trigger. In today's multipolar world, driven in the long run more by economic than military imperatives, the finger that writes the rules is the one with real power. Anne Marie Slaughter, dean of the Princeton School of International Affairs, gives a name to the figures that are the unsung forces behind this twenty-first-cen-tury shift. "Regulators are the new diplomats," Slaughter writes in her book *A New World Order*, "on the front lines of issues that were once the exclusive preserve of domestic policy, but that now cannot be resolved by national authorities alone."[7]

Regulations might seem the realm of paper-pushing bureau-crats—hardly the realm of glamorous diplomacy—but it is here where clashes over values ripple through the international system. Globalization was supposed to bring greater uniformity to the rules governing the flow of capital and labor, and to a great extent it has done so. But few of the architects of that system, and fewer still among its many critics—who appeared on the streets of Seattle or Montreal or Doha in the hundreds of thousands—could have imagined that regulations protecting citizens might actually be made stronger. More rigorous criteria for assessing the long-term sustainability and health impacts of today's chemical and technological creations are being established with the backup of consumers in the world's largest single market. This trend threatens to leave American industry trailing their increasingly "green" European competitors.

The EU is moving these policies forward within the constraints imposed by the World Trade Organization, premier arbiter of the values that lie behind economic conflict. The United States, were it to choose to do so, would be compelled to do the same. The main aim of the WTO and its predecessor, the Global Agreement on Tariffs and Trade (GATT), has been to create a harmonized global system for the free flow of capital and goods, detouring what are considered to be the parochial and unpredictable interests of individual nations. Until now, the primary impact of free trade principles has been to drive protective standards downward toward the lowest common denominator. That system rests on a sequence of critical precedents which, over time, have come to be interpreted as expressing the principle that environmental protection in one country constitutes discrimination against another. It is a highly selective supermarket of goods and ideas.

To a trade lawyer, for example, "dolphin-tuna" signifies not an unusual seafood dining experience but the principle established by the WTO that one country does not have the right to protect species in its waters from the predations of foreign fishermen (a decision in favor of Mexico's efforts to block U.S. protection of dolphins, which are caught in those tuna nets). "Genetically modified organisms" are not those mixtures of genes showing up in our food, but the principle that governments cannot issue a blanket ban on an entire class of products without identifying individual risks. "Beef hormones" are not something to be avoided if you are a fan of organic meat, but the principle that one country cannot ban the ingredients in food from another country without substantial scientific evidence to back it up; the EU lost that challenge by the United States in 1988 at the GATT, but rather than comply has opted to pay about one hundred million dollars a year in penalties on exports to the United States to keep growth-stimulating hormones out of European beef.

One of the most significant trade decisions, however, has spun a different way in the long haul of history. Back in 1979, when the EU was the European Community, the European Court of Justice decided on the fate of an obscure French liqueur called "Cassis de Dijon," a drink most commonly used in the mixing of kir royale cocktails. On the surface "Cassis" looks amusingly simple: it prevented Germany from requiring that all liqueurs have an alcohol content of at least 25 percent, which the court found unfairly excluded competition from the French crème de cassis, which has 15 percent. But that decision took on seminal importance in the evolution of the EU, establishing the principle that no member state could discriminate against the import of goods from another member state.[8] Fallout from "Cassis" rolled first through Europe, laying the legal ground for what is now an integrated, half-billion-person-strong, single market. Nearly three decades later, the fallout is roiling through the world as that market, represented by the EU, presents a historic challenge to the United States.

Every European diplomat I've spoken with has been careful to insist that Europe is not trying to impose its will on the United

States. Much like America once did, Europe is writing new rules—and leaving it up to potential partners to decide whether to pay the ticket of admission to its lucrative markets. "We are not imposing our standards on America," commented Camilo-Barcia Garcia, a veteran of the European Commission who negotiated entry into the Union by several countries, including his native Spain. Most recently, he served as the Spanish consul in San Francisco. "But if American companies want to be active in the European market, they must take account of European rules. We are making foreign companies respect our standards when they are in Europe."[9] This diplomatic language is new to the transatlantic relationship, though its inversion has certainly been true for decades.

Americans felt few of the effects when it was they who wrote the rules. Now someone else is writing many of these rules. This is what Penelope Naas, formerly of the Commerce Department (who we met in chapter 1) was referring to when she commented that "things are going to get tough" for U.S. manufacturers.[10]

By sculpting their laws to conform to the nondiscriminatory requirements of the WTO—applying the same standards to European and foreign producers—the European Union is showing how standards for environmental and other protections may be leveraged upward rather than down. America's architects of the WTO-centered trade regime now have to live with the results.

The European Union's environmental reforms suggest a way out of a deadlock that has been repeated countless times in the United States, with a repetition that has taken on qualities of kabuki theatre. Environmental advocates demand the removal of toxins or ask for greater energy efficiency; industry and government claim that it is unrealistic, that we must become accustomed to trade-offs in order to enjoy our modern conveniences.

Europe is calling that bluff by demonstrating that these are false trade-offs. What Americans have been told is impossible is happening. From cosmetics to appliances, industrial chemicals to toys, the Europeans are demonstrating that there are alternatives by creating legal and financial incentives for industry to create them. The EU estimates that its new environmental directives have spurred into being billions of dollars in new "greener" industries and technology. In Europe, "green chemists" have been encouraged to develop more benign alternatives to the thousands of toxic chemicals on the market today. The limitations on energy use agreed to by the signatories of the Kyoto accord have given a huge boost to European development of more efficient technology and alternative energy sources like wind and solar, which are growing yearly in the double digits and offering new export markets, while helping reduce greenhouse gas emissions.

By contrast, the United States was arguing against change at a time when citizens on both continents were calling for greater environmental sensitivity in the marketplace. As C. Boyden Gray was gearing up for his debut ambassadorial assault on REACH, the pages of leading business journals—*Business Week*, *Fortune*, the *Financial Times* and others—were filled with predictions that the next big growth area of the economy was "green technology."

Substitutes already exist for at least 25 percent of "problematic chemicals," according to estimates by the Center for Sustainable Production at the University of Massachusetts–Lowell (UML), the leading U.S. research center for what has come to be known as "green chemistry." Another 45 percent are showing great promise at UML and other materials labs around the world. "The reason that we don't have even more alternatives is that green chemistry has not yet matured as a science," commented John Warner, director of the Warner Babcock Institute for Green Chemistry, which develops commercial applications for those less toxic alternatives. "Chemists are trained to create new molecules. . . . We've gotten pretty good at identifying problems with chemicals, whether the combination of molecules creates carcinogens or neurotoxins. But what we're not doing is talking about how to make that molecule not do that." By making comparative toxicity data available to the public and by edging the most dangerous substances off the market, the Europeans are providing an important stimulus for that research, Warner said. "The function of government is to offer incentives through regulations. That way, the new research becomes part of the cost structure."[11]

The United States is already losing ground to Europe in the chemical business, slipping over the course of the last decade from a surplus to a more than five billion dollar deficit in its chemical trade with Europe.[12] That trade deficit, predicts Mike Wilson, the environmental health scientist at University of California–Berkeley's School of Public Health, will increase as the market for U.S.–produced "basic chemicals"—a menu of substances that has changed little in thirty years—diminishes under the public glare offered by REACH and as consumers' sensitivity to environmental consequences increases. "The Europeans are already gaining an advantage over us in clean technology," said Wilson. "As the market shifts, that will put them into an advantageous situation."[13]

Michael Kirschner, the design engineer who now specializes in bringing his high-tech clients up to speed with the new European and Chinese regulations governing electronics, told me that 80 to 90 percent of the changes his industry has been forced to make were, as he put it, "relatively easy. . . . They were done in a non-manpower-intensive manner." Alternatives, he said, were available for the chemicals now banned.[14] The United States had never asked, so they had never before looked.

By February 2007 the REACH road show hit America's shores—but this road show was born in Washington D.C., not in Brussels. In that month, the Department of Commerce held a seminar for businesses in Charlotte, North Carolina, to explain how to comply with REACH.[15] It was the first of a series of seminars to be held with

American industry across the country. In the same month, the Defense Department's procurement division participated in a three-day session in Monterey, California, to educate contractors about the chemicals in their military hardware being used on U.S. bases in Europe.[16] After fighting the Europeans for five years, the U.S. government was now impelled to teach Americans how to comply with EU laws intended to protect their citizens back home. At the same time, many American states, which have given up on finding leadership in Washington, are looking to Brussels for ideas on environmental reform. "I'm getting calls all the time from our members asking, 'Has the EU banned this, has the EU banned that,' so they can act next," says Adam Schafer, director of the National Conference of Environmental Legislators, representing state-level political legisla-tors.[17] California, Massachusetts, and New York have begun imple-menting elements of REACH into their state regulations; other states, such as Maine and Washington, have cited Europe's prece-dent in their efforts to ban particular chemicals.

There is, however, a troubling side to this transformative process. By dismantling the barriers of national prerogative, globalization instead granted prerogatives to the powers of the market. The EU offers an example of the power that can be wielded in the realm of the environment. But the market can cut both or in multiple ways. It is inherently undemocratic.

David Wirth, who was on the State Department team that negoti-ated the Montreal Protocol in 1988 and is now the head of interna-tional law at Boston College, has been following developments in Europe with a mixture of satisfaction—the EU is taking actions he has long advocated from inside and outside government—as well as trepidation for the implications for American democracy.

"If California or some other state adopts an EU directive, then who cares what EPA says anymore?" Wirth commented. "If you're not engaged in the process, then you can't influence the outcome. . . . The idea that environmental regulations in the United States are a response to the European Union means that we, as Americans, are getting policies that are a result not of politics or democratic input [in America], but the product of politics and the market in Europe."[18]

The Bush administration's abnegation of environmental leadership has ceded this terrain to more forward-looking forces in Brussels. Despite efforts by C. Boyden Gray and others speaking for U.S. industry, who have been jolted into an awareness of Brussels' potent global presence, Americans are left with little control over policies that are coming rapidly home to roost in their kitchens, their offices, their boudoirs, and their garages. As Michael Kirschner put it to me, "By aggressively refusing to come up with any forward-thinking solutions, industry ends up with RoHS from Europe in California. And if they offer no solutions to the problems with TSCA, the same thing will happen, over which they'll have no control."

Power has shifted. In the process, American citizens are being put in a position that would have been unimaginable a decade ago: in some instances a dumping ground for goods not wanted elsewhere in the world, in other instances the accidental beneficiaries of protective standards created by another government over which they have no influence. The question is whether the United States will rediscover what Stacy Vandeveer's students barely knew that it had lost. There is one thing that those students can be sure of: The United States is no longer where it likes to imagine itself to be, at the center of a universe around which the rest of the world revolves.

NOTES

Chapter 1

1) Interview and tour of Quanta Labs, with Terry Liu, the son of the company's president, February 9, 2006. The workshop was sponsored by the high-tech consulting firm Ops a la Carte.
2) Global Supply Chain Program, Arrow Green Solutions, an environmental consulting firm based in the UK, Power Point presentation, June 9, 2005.
3) Third National Report on Human Exposure to Environmental Chemicals, Centers for Disease Control and Prevention, 2005. http://www.cdc.gov/exposurereport/pdf/thirdreport.pdf
4) Fertile Grounds for Inquiry: Environmental Effects on Human Reproduction, *Environmental Health Perspectives*, vol. 114, no. 11, November, 2006, pg. 646.
5) The EU's GDP was $13.5 trillion in 2005, according to the International Monetary Fund; that same year the U.S. GDP was $13 trillion, according to the Bureau of Economic Analysis in the Department of Commerce.
6) "Trade Issues: Mercosur," European Commission, DG-External Trade, update as of June, 2006; and "Integration and Trade in the Americas," Inter-American Development Bank, December 2004.
7) Interview with David Vogel, at UC Berkeley, November 7, 2006.
8) Interview with David Wirth, at Vermont Law School, South Royalton, VT, July 22, 2004.
9) Telephone interview with Becky Linder, in Washington, DC, September 7, 2006.
10) Interview with Mike Wilson, Berkeley, CA, October 3, 2006.
11) *Circle of Poison: Pesticides and People in a Hungry World*, David Weir and Mark Schapiro, Institute for Food and Development Policy, 1981.
12) Background source material on history of the European Union includes: *Jean Monnet: The Path to European Unity*, edited by Douglas Brinkley and Clifford Hackett, St. Martin's Press, 1991; and *The United States of Europe: The New Superpower and the End of American Supremacy*, T.R. Reid, Penguin Press, 2004; *The European Dream*, Jeremy Rifkin, JP Tarcher/Penguin, 2004.
13) Interview with Bo Manderup Jensen, in the European Parliament, Brussels, June 9, 2004.
14) Interview with Frank Schwalba-Hoth, in Brussels, June, 25, 2005.
15) Interview with Robert Donkers, in Washington, DC, March 9, 2006.
16) "U.S. Department of Commerce Names Standards Liaison," announcement by U.S. Dept. of Commerce, International Trade Administration, September 12, 2003.
17) Interview with Penelope Naas, in Washington, DC, September 21, 2006.

Chapter 2

1) Interview with Joris Pollet, at Procter & Gamble headquarters in Brussels, October 13, 2005.
2) Environmental Working Group, "Skin Deep," http://www.cosmeticdatabase.com/research/whythismatters.php
3) "State of the Evidence: What Is the Connection Between the Environment and Breast Cancer?" Breast Cancer Fund, 2006, pg. 4. http://www.breastcancerfund.org
4) Use of Hair Dyes and Bladder Cancer Risk, Manuela Gago-Dominguez and four co-authors affiliated with the Dept. of Preventative Medicine, USC/Norris Comprehensive Cancer Center, *International Journal of Cancer*, vol. 91, issue 4, February 2001, pp: 575-579.

5) "Cancer-Causing Chemicals: A Thousand Threats. Cancer-causing chemicals don't work alone, but in tandem. A scientist argues for increased vigilance," Devra Davis, *Newsweek International*, March 5, 2007.

That article reflects scientific findings in: "Personal Care Products that contain estrogens or xenoestrogens may increase breast cancer risk," Devra L. Davis and a team of co-authors affiliated with the Center for Environmental Oncology at the University of Pittsburgh Cancer Institute, the Epidemiology Center for Cancer Prevention in Bordeaux, France, the NYU Clinical Cancer Center and the Center for Research on Minority Health at the University of Texas, *Medical Hypotheses*, vol. 68, no. 4, 2007, pp: 756-766.

6) Directive 2003/15/EC of the European Parliament and of the Council of 27 February 2003 amending Council Directive 76/768/EEC on the approximation of the laws of the Member States relating to cosmetic products (otherwise known as the 7th amendment to the Cosmetics Directive, which came into force on March 1, 2005), published in the Official Journal of the European Union, March 11, 2003.

7) "Comparative Study on Cosmetics Legislation in the EU and other Principal Markets with Special Attention to so-called Borderline Products," Final Report, prepared by Risk and Policy Analysis, Ltd, London, England for the European Commission, DG Enterprise, August 2004. EU guidelines for information on cosmetics: http://www.ec.europa.eu/enterprise/cosmetics/doc/guide_access_info.pdf

8) Telephone interview with Charlotte Brody, in San Francisco, July 26, 2006.

9) "FDA Authority over Cosmetics," http://www.cfsan.fda.gov/~dms/cos-206.html

10) Cosmetic Ingredient Review Board: http://www.cir-safety.org. A comprehensive article written for the American Academy of Dermatology by members of the review board explains the board's methods for assessing cosmetic ingredient safety: Safety of Ingredients Used in Cosmetics, Wilma Bergfeld, Donald Belsito, James Marks and F. Alan Anderson, Journal of the American Academy of Dermatology, January, 2005.

11) National Library of Medicine, Household Products Database: http://household products.nlm.nih.gov/cgi-bin/household/brands?tbl=chem&id=10

12) "The Hare and the Tortoise Revisited: The New Politics of Consumer and Environmental Regulation in Europe," David Vogel, British Journal of Political Science, vol 33, 2003, pp: 567-568.

13) Environmental Working Group, "Skin Deep." http://www.cosmeticdatabase.com/research/whythismatters.php

14) Telephone interview with Jane Houlihan, in Washington, April 27, 2007.

15) Telephone interview with John Bailey, in New York City, April 10, 2007.

16) Scientific committee opinions can be accessed at: http://europa.eu.int/comm/health/ph_risk/committees/sccp/sccp_opinions_en.htm

17) Environmental Working Group, "Skin Deep." http://www.cosmeticdatabase.com/research/whythismatters.php

18) Telephone interview with Tim Long, Cincinnati, OH, December 7, 2006.

19) Telephone interview with Francine Lamoriello, in New York City, April 10, 2007.

20) Telephone interview with Tim Long, Cincinnati, OH, April 5, 2007.

21) Lobbying contributions compiled by the California Secretary of State. http://calaccess.ss.ca.gov/Lobbying/Employers/Detail.aspx?id=1144084&session= 2005&view=activity

22) Advocates of the Safe Cosmetics Act: www.safecosmetics.org; Opponents of the Safe Cosmetics Act: www.cosmeticsaresafe.org.

23) Senate Health Committee, on videotape, April 20, 2005.

24) Telephone interview with Janet Nudelman, in San Francisco, CA, November 3, 2005.

25) Calculation based on financial figures from Google Finance, December 19, 2006.

26) Powder Flies as Backers, Foes Press Positions on Cosmetics Bill, by Marjorie Lundstrom, Sacramento Bee, September 29, 2005

27) The 1791 case is cited in, Un-Making Law:The Conservative Campaign to Roll Back the Common Law, Jay M. Feinman, Beacon Press, 2004, p: 42.

28) The Chamber of Commerce's $100 million judicial campaigns are described in a deposition of Rob Engstrom, a vice president for political affairs at the Institute for Legal Reform, a political arm of the U.S. Chamber of Commerce. His testimony was part of a case brought in October, 2005 to the Public Disclosure Commission of Washington state by Public Citizen and the Seattle University School of Law alleging improper campaign donations by the Chamber to state-wide judicial campaigns.

29) "The Corporate Lobbying Campaign in Favor of the Class Action Bills (H.R. 1875/S. 353)," Public Citizen, September 23, 1999. http://www.citizen.org/congress/civjus/archive/classaction/articles.cfm?ID=541

30) Procter & Gamble Fund, 990 Forms for Internal Revenue Service, July 1, 2003-June 30, 2004 and July 1, 2004-June 30, 2005.

31) "Lawsuits target Ford SuperCab roof," and "European vehicles exceed standard for U.S. car roofs," Jeff Plungis and Bill Vlasic, Special Report in the Detroit News, April 12, 2004; also, "Memos: Ford made Explorer roof weaker," Jeff Plungis, Detroit News, March 29, 2005.

32) Telephone interview with Derek Johnson, in Eugene, OR, April 14, 2006.

33) Interview with David Wirth, in Boston, November 2, 2006.

Chapter 3

1) "Toys and Chemical Safety, A Thought Starter," presented at Fifth Session of the Intergovernmental Forum on Chemical Safety, Budapest, Hungary, 25-29 September, 2006.

2) Perinatal Exposure to the Phthalates DEHP, BBP, and DINP, but not DEP, DMP, or DOTP, Alters Sexual Differentiation of the Male Rat, L. Earl Gray, et al., *Toxicological Sciences*, vol. 58, December, 2000, pp. 350-365.

A Mixture of the 'Anti-Androgens' Linuron and Butyl Benzene Phthalate Alters Sexual Differentiation of the Male Rat in a Cumulative Fashion, L. Earl Gray and six co-authors affiliated with the EPA's National Health and Environmental Effects Research Laboratory and North Carolina State University, Raleigh, *Biology of Reproduction*, vol. 71, October 2004.

Dr. Gray's work has also been incorporated in several EPA risk assessments of DEHP; his most recent contribution to the scientific literature on the relation between phthalates and male reproductive development is:

Cumulative Effects of Dibutyl Phthalate and Diethylhexyl Phthalate on Male Rat Reproductive Tract Development: Altered Fetal Steroid Hormones and Genes, L. Earl Gray and five co-authors affiliated with the EPA's National Health and Environmental Research Laboratory, Raleigh, NC, *Toxicological Sciences*, March 30, 2007. http://toxsci.oxfordjournals.org/cgi/content/abstract/kfm069v1

For background information on rates of male sexual malformations and their possible links to chemical exposure, also see:

The Relationship between Environmental Exposures to Phthalates and DNA Damage in Human Sperm Using the Neutral Comet Assay, Susan M. Duty and six co-authors affiliated with the National Institute of Environmental Health Sciences, Dept. of Health and Human Services, *Environmental Health Perspectives*, December, 2002, and International Trends in Rates of Hypospadias and Cryptorchidism, Leonard J. Paulozzi of the National Center for Environmental Health, Centers for Disease Control, *Environmental Health Perspectives*, vol. 107, no. 4, April, 1999.

3) Telephone interview with L. Earl Gray, in Durham, NC, February 7, 2006.

4) "Decrease in Anogenital Distance among Male Infants with Prenatal Phthalate Exposure," Shanna H. Swan (and ten co-authors), Environmental Health Perspectives, vol. 113, no. 8, August 2005.

5) Use of Di(2-Ethylhexyl) Phthalate-Containing Medical Products and Urinary Levels of Mono(2-Ethylhexyl) Phthalate in Neonatal Intensive Care Unit Infants, Ronald Green and six co-authors affiliated with the Harvard School of Public Health, the Centers for Disease Control and the Science and Environmental Health Network, *Environmental Health Perspectives*, vol. 113, no. 9, September 2005, pp. 1222-1225.

6) Monograph on the Potential Human Reproductive and Developmental Effects of Di(2-Ethylhexyl) Phthalate (DEHP), National Toxicology Program, Center for the Evaluation of Risks to Human Reproduction, U.S. Department of Health and Human Services, November 2006

7) FDA recommendation can be found at: http://www.fda.gov/cdrh/safety/dehp.html

8) "ANA and Health Care Without Harm Urge Hospitals and Health Care Professionals to Switch to DEHP-Free Medical Devices," Press release by American Nurses Association, January 19, 2007.

And interview with Marion Condon, Sr. Staff Specialist at American Nurses Association, in Silver Spring, Maryland, March 9, 2007.

For a comprehensive survey of phthalates in medical devices in Europe and the United States, see: "PVC in Medical Devices," a joint report by Karolinska University Hospital in Sweden and the U.S.-based NGO, Health Care Without Harm, 30 June, 2005.

9) Telephone interview with Shanna Swan, in Rochester, NY, January 22, 2006.

10) For criticism of Swan's work, see the website of the Phthalate Esters Panel: http://www.phthalates.org/. Also, see *Science* magazine: Panel Finds No Proof that Phthalates Harm Infant Reproductive System, Jocelyn Kaiser, vol. 310, 21 October 2005.

For criticism of agd as a marker of gender, and Swan's response, see *Environmental Health Perspectives*, vol. 114, no. 1, January 2006, letter from Gerald N. McEwen, Jr. of the Cosmetic, Toiletry and Fragrance Association and Gerald Renner, of the European Cosmetic, Toiletry and Perfume Association, "Validity of Anogenital Distance as a Marker of *in Utero* Phthalate Exposure and Author's Response." Swan's response follows in the same issue of *Environmental Health Perspectives*.

11) Interview with Joan Lawrence after Health Committee hearing, January 10, 2006.

12) This study was cited by Dr. David Cadogan, Senior Scientist at the Confederation of European Chemical Industries, in an interview at the chemical industry trade group's headquarters in Brussels, October 13, 2005.

13) Human Breast Milk Contamination with Phthalates and Alterations of Endogenous Reproductive Hormones in Infants Three Months of Age, Niels E. Skakkebaek and Katharina M. Main, and eleven other researchers affiliated with the University Department of Growth and Reproduction, Rigshospitalet, Copenhagen, Denmark; the Dept. of Physiology and Pediatrics, University of Turku, Turku, Finland; and the Dept of Biostatistics, University of Copenhagen, Copenhagen, Denmark. *Environmental Health Perspectives*, vol. 114, no. 2, February 2006.

14) *In Utero* Exposure to Di-2-Ethylhexyl Phthalate and Duration of Human Pregnancy, Giuseppe Latini, Claudio De Felice, Giuseppe Presta, Antonio Del Vecchio, Irma Paris, Fabrizio Ruggieri and Pietro Mazzeo, *Environmental Health Perspectives*, vol. 111, no. 14, November 2003. (Research sponsored by Clinical Physiology Institute, National Research Council of Italy, Brindisi, Italy.)

15) "Opinion on Phthalate migration from soft-PVC toys and child-care articles—Data made available since the 16th of June 1998, opinion expressed at the 6th CSTEE plenary meeting," European Chemicals Bureau, November 26/27, 1998.

16) "WWF Chemical Testing Reveals Contamination of European Lawmakers," World Wildlife Fund (Press Release), April 21, 2004.

17) Directive 2005/84/EC of the European Parliament and of the Council, 14 December 2005, amending for the 22nd time Council Directive 76/769/EEC on the approximation

of the laws, regulations and administrative provisions of the Member States relating to restrictions on the marketing and use of certain dangerous substances and preparations (phthalates in toys and childcare articles).

18) "Risk Reduction Strategy: Bis (2-Etylhexyl) Phthalate3, DEHP," January 2003, conducted by the Swedish National Chemicals Directorate on behalf of the Scientific Committee on Toxicity, Ecotoxicity and the Environment (CSTEE) of the European Commission's Directorate General for Health and Consumer Protection, January, 2003.

19) "Expert Panel Update on the Reproductive and Developmental Toxicity of Di (2-Ethylhexyl) Phthalate," National Toxicology Program, Center for the Evaluation of Risks to Human Reproduction, November, 2005, pg. 179.

20) Telephone interview with Shanna Swan, in Rochester, NY, October 31, 2006.

21) "Why Poison Ourselves? A Precautionary Approach to Synthetic Chemicals," Anne Platt McGinn, Worldwatch Paper #153, Worldwatch Institute, 2000, pg. 59.

22) Phthalate Exposure and Human Semen Parameters, Susan M. Duty and Russ Hauser of the Harvard School of Public Health, *Epidemiology*, vol. 14, 2003, pp. 269-277.

23) "Expert Panel Update on the Reproductive and Developmental Toxicity of Di (2-Ethylhexyl) Phthalate," National Toxicology Program, Center for the Evaluation of Risks to Human Reproduction, November 2005, pg. 180.

24) "Third National Report on Human Exposure to Environmental Chemicals, National Center for Environmental Health, Centers for Disease Control and Prevention, July 2005, pp: 269-271.

25) Monograph on the Potential Human Reproductive and Developmental Effects of Di (2-Ethylhexyl) Phthalate (DEHP), National Toxicology Program, Center for the Evaluation of Risks to Human Reproduction, November 2006, pg. vii.

Other studies on phthalate exposure reviewed by the author include:

Decreased Serum Free Testosterone in Workers Exposed to High Levels of De-n-butyl Phthalate (DBP) and Di-2-Ethylhexyl Phthalate (DEHP): A Cross Sectional Study in China," Environmental Health Perspectives, vol. 114, no. 11, November, 2006.

Pediatric Exposure and Potential Toxicity of Phthalate Plasticizers, Katherine M. Shea, MD, MPH, in *Pediatrics* (Official Journal of the American Academy of Pediatrics), vol. 111, no. 6, June, 2003, pp. 1467-1474.

Male Reproductive Effects of Phthalates: An Emerging Picture, Jane A. Hoppin, *Epidemiology*, vol. 14, 2003, pp. 259-260.

For a comprehensive journalistic treatment of rising concern over phthalates in toys, see:

From an Ingredient in Cosmetics, Toys, A Safety Concern: Male Reproductive Development Is Issue With Phthalates, Used in Host of Products, Peter Waldman, *Wall Street Journal*, October 4, 2005, page A1.

26) "Decreased Serum Free Testosterone in Workers Exposed to High Levels of Di-n-butyl Phthalate (DBP) and Di-2-ethylhexyl Phthalate (DEHP): A Cross-Sectional Study in China," by Guowei Pan at the Dept of Environmental Epidemiology, Liaoning Provincial Center for Disease Prevention and Control, China, and a team of researchers affiliated with the National Cancer Center in Tokyo, Japan; Research Center for Cancer Prevention and Screening, National Cancer Center, Tokyo, Japan; Department of Environmental Epidemiology, University of Occupational and Environmental Health, Kitakyushu, Japan; Department of Hygiene and Preventive Medicine, Showa University, School of Medicine, Tokyo, Japan; Department of Infectious Disease, Shenyang Municipal Center for Disease Prevention and Control, Shenyang, China; and Department of Analytical Chemistry, Faculty of Pharmaceutical Sciences, Hoshi University, Tokyo, Japan, published in *Environmental Health Perspectives*, vol. 114, no. 11, November, 2006.

27) Interview with Joel Tickner at Boston Chemicals Conference.

28) The CPSC's decision not to restrict phthalates in toys was issued on February 26, 2003 in the form of a letter from Todd A. Stevenson, CPSC Secretary, to Jeffrey Becker Wise, Policy Director of the National Environmental Trust, Re: 'Petition Requesting Ban of Polyvinyl Chloride (PVC) in Products Intended for Children under Five Years of Age and Under.' This letter is available on the CPSC website: www.cpsc.gov.
Also, see: Young Children and Plastic Toys, *Consumer Product Safety Review* (a CPSC newsletter), pp. 3-5, Summer, 2003.

29) Telephone interview with Scott Wolfson, Deputy Director of Public Affairs, CPSC, in Washington, DC, November 3, 2005.

30) Plasticiser 2006 conference, in Brussels, January 24-25, 2006, "Program Overview."

31) E-mail from William Pagano to author, November 20, 2006.

32) Toy Industries of Europe: www.tietoy.org

33) U.S. Department of Commerce and U.S. International Trade Commission, "All Toys, Games and Dolls: U.S. Domestic Exports," year to year data from 1996 to 2006. The three percent growth figure is based on Commerce Dept. statistics for sales in Europe's biggest individual markets: France, Germany, Italy, the Netherlands, Spain, and the United Kingdom.

34) E-mail from John Taylor, Arcadia Investment Corporation, to my researcher, Samuel Schramski, February 24, 2006.

35) Telephone interview with a toy analyst who requested anonymity, August 22, 2006.

36) Telephone interview with Shanna Swan, in Rochester, NY, January 22, 2006.

37) Letter from Fermin Cuza, Senior Vice President at Mattel, Inc. to William M. Daley, Secretary of Commerce, March 9, 1998, obtained from an FOIA request by Joseph diGangi of the Science and Environmental Health Network.

38) Letter from Vice President Al Gore to Representative Henry Waxman, December 21, 1998.

39) Follow-up telephone interview with Joan Lawrence, in New York City, November 15, 2006.

40) Chemical analysis of playthings is cited in: *The Right Start: The Need to Eliminate Toxic Chemicals from Baby Products*, U.S. PIRG Education Fund and Environment California, October 2005.

41) Telephone interview with Pete Price, in Sacramento, CA, November 4, 2005.

42) For more on the Weinberg Group, see: The Weinberg Proposal: A scientific consulting firm says that it aids companies in trouble, but critics say that it manufactures uncertainty and undermines science, by Paul D. Thacker, *Environmental Science and Technology*, February 22, 2006. http://pubs.acs.org/subscribe/journals/esthag-w/2006/feb/business/pt_weinberg.html

43) Interview with James Lamb, after a state Health Committee hearing, Sacramento, CA, January 10, 2006.

44) Interview with David Cadogan, at CEFIC headquarters in Brussels, October 13, 2005.
(In 2007, Dr. Cadogan left CEFIC to become the Director of the European Council for Plasticisers and Intermediates.)

45) RAPEX can be accessed on the Web, offering a week by week survey of citations and confiscations due to violations of EU safety standards. References to goods prohibited due to their phthalate content are at:
http:// ec.europa.eu/consumers/dyna/rapex/create_rapex.cfm?rx_id=83, citation # 8
http://ec.europa.eu/consumers/dyna/rapex/create_rapex.cfm?rx_id=86, citation # 15.

46) Toxic. San Francisco Prepares to Ban Certain Chemicals in Products for Tots, but Enforcement Will Be Tough—and Toymakers Question Necessity, Jane Kay, *San Francisco Chronicle*, November 19, 2006. (This article includes test results on toys.)

47) Telephone interview with June Weintraub, Epidemiologist with the San Francisco Dept. of Public Health, Environmental Health Section, May10, 2007; also see: Firms Sue Over Ban on Use of Chemicals: Manufacturers Team with Toymakers to Challenge S.F. Law, Jane Kay, *San Francisco Chronicle*, November 18, 2006.

Chapter 4

1) For the text of the Stockholm Convention on Persistent Organic Pollutants (POPS), latest ratifications, etc., see: www.pops.int. For information on U.S. and POPS, see: www.uspopswatch.org.
2) "President, Secretary of State Colin Powell, and EPA Administrator Christine Todd Whitman Discuss Health and the Environment," news release and transcript from the White House, April 19, 2001.
3) Letter from William Moschella, Assistant Attorney General, to Senator Tom Harkin, March 25, 2004.
4) "Validity of Provisions Mandating Notice and Comment Proceedings in Response to the Decisions of Parties Operating Pursuant to International Conventions and Protocols," memorandum sent by T. J. Halstead, Legislative Attorney in the American Law Division of the Congressional Research Service to Senator Tom Harkin, March 30, 2004.
5) Telephone interview with Kristin Schafer, in San Francisco, CA, March 14, 2006.
6) Telephone interview with Janice Jensen, in Washington, DC, March 29, 2006.
7) Telephone interview with a congressional aide who requested anonymity, March 1, 2006.
8) "Proposal to add a new substance to the Stockholm Convention on Persistent Organic Pollutants (POPS)," formal submission nominating lindane from Daniel Chacon Anaya, Director for Integrated Management of Materials and Risky Activities in Mexico's Secretariat for Environment and Natural Resources, paperwork formally submitted on June 29, 2005.
9) "Lindane and other HCH Isomers—EPA Risk Assessment Fact Sheet," EPA, February 8, 2006. http://www.epa.gov/pesticides/reregistration/ REDs/factsheets/lindane_isomers_fs.htm
10) FDA recommendations on use of lindane: http://www.fda.gov/cder/drug/infopage/lindane/default.htmFA
11) Telephone interview with Mario Yarto, in Mexico City, April 8, 2006.
12) "Nomination Dossier for Lindane: Submission by the United States to the Working Group of the Sound Management of Chemicals (SMOC) to consider lindane as a candidate substance for development of a NARAP" (National Regional Action Plan), submitted to the Council on Environmental Cooperation, January 15, 1999.
13) Telephone interview with Luke Trip, in Montreal, Canada, July 27, 2005.
14) Letter from Edwin L. Johnson, Senior Consultant to the Technology Sciences Group, Charles A. O'Connor, III, and Michael Boucher, Counsel to the Crompton Corporation (formulators of lindane) to Michael Goodis, Branch Chief of the EPA's Special Review and Registration Division, arguing in favor of EPA's reregistration of lindane, August 3, 2004.
   Johnson served in the EPA's Office of Pesticide Programs for more than fifteen years, before becoming a Senior Consultant to the Technology Sciences Group, a lobbying firm that advises companies on regulatory matters, upon leaving the agency.
15) "Mexico to Eliminate Toxic Chemical Lindane," Commission for Environmental Cooperation release, October 8, 2004; also, telephone interview with Mario Yarto.
16) Circle of Poison: Pesticides and People in a Hungry World, David Weir and Mark Schapiro, Institute for Food and Development Policy, 1981.
17) "Lindane and Other HCH Isomers—EPA Risk Assessment Fact Sheet," February 8, 2006.
18) Telephone interview with Fernando Bejarano, in Mexico City, September 2, 2005.
19) Letter from Condoleeza Rice and Stephen L. Johnson to Senator Bill Frist, July 22, 2005.
20) "Lindane Voluntary Cancellation and RED Addendum Fact Sheet," EPA, July 2006.
21) "Addendum to the 2002 Lindane Reregistration Eligibility Decision," EPA, July 2006.
22) Telephone interview with Daryl Ditz, in Washington, DC, October 4, 2006.

23) "ToxFAQ's for Polybrominated Diphenyl Ethers (PBDEs)," Agency for Toxic Substances and Disease Registry, September, 2004; also, "Draft Risk Profile prepared by the ad hoc working group on Pentabromodiphenyl Ether under the Persistent Organic Pollutant Review Committee of the Stockholm Convention," August, 2006.
24) Claudia McMurray's testimony to the House Energy and Commerce Committee, Subcommittee on Environment and Hazardous Materials, March 6, 2006.
25) "U.S. Ratification of the Stockholm Convention: Analysis of Pending POPS Legislation," Center for International Environmental Law, February 28, 2006.
26) Telephone interview with Barbara Perthen-Palmisiano, in Vienna, Austria, October 5, 2006.
27) *Against the Gods: The Remarkable Story of Risk*, Peter L. Bernstein, John Wiley & Sons, 1998, pg. 1.
28) Interview with Thomas McKone in his office at UC Berkeley, April 6, 2006.

Chapter 5

1) Tribunal de Grande Instance d'Orleans, Jugement Correctionnel du 9 Decembre, 2005, no. de jugement 2345/S3/2005. The case was between Monsanto (La Societe Monsanto) and Francois DuFour, a local farmer, and 47 others. Translation of decision by author. Also see, Activists Destruction of GM Crops Was Justified: French Court, Agence France Presse, December 9, 2005.
2) USDA Foreign Agricultural Service, Global Agriculture Information Network (GAIN), December 14, 2005 and July 28, 2006. (The USDA tracks the threats to biotechnology around the world, as well as other agriculture-related news.)
3) Telephone interview with Christopher Horner, in St. Louis, MO, March 22, 2006.
4) I visited Laura Krause's farm in August, 2002 with a film crew from the PBS news-magazine program NOW With Bill Moyers. The story was broadcast on October 4, 2002—entitled Seeds of Conflict—and a print version, "Sowing Disaster?," was later published in the October 28, 2002 issue of *The Nation*. http://www.thenation.com/doc/20021028/schapiro
5) "Managing 'Pollen Drift' to Minimize Contamination of Non-GMO Corn," Ohio State University Extension Fact Sheet, AGF-153-04.
6) Telephone interview with Laura Krause, in Mt. Vernon, Iowa, December 19, 2005.
7) *Gone to Seed: Transgenic Contaminants in the Traditional Seed Supply*, Union of Concerned Scientists, 2004.
8) "Impossible Coexistence," published by Greenpeace, Spain on April 4, 2006.
9) http://www.gmcontaminationregister.org/
10) "Adoption of Genetically Engineered Crops in the U.S.: Corn Varieties and Soybean Varieties," USDA Economic Research Service, 2000-2006.
11) Going to 'Great Lengths' to Prevent the Escape of Genes that Produce Specialty Chemicals, Norman Ellstrand, *Plant Physiology*, vol. 132, August 2003, pp. 1770-1774; "Statement of the Scientific Panel on Genetically Modified Organisms on an evaluation of the 13-week rat feeding study on MON 863 maize, submitted by the German authorities to the European Commission," 20 October 2004; Stalk Raving Mad: French Farmers, Activists Battle Over Rise in Genetically Altered Corn, John W. Miller, *Wall Street Journal*, October 12, 2006; Sowing Disaster? How Genetically Altered Corn Has Altered the Global Landscape, Mark Schapiro, *The Nation*, October 28, 2002.
12) Interview with Karin Scheele, in European Parliament, Brussels, October 10, 2005.
13) The WTO's official decision was rendered in September, 2006; a summary of the findings and history of the case is described at: http://www.wto.org/english/tratop_e/dispu_e/cases_e/ds293_e.htm There also were numerous press reports of a preliminary opinion issued in February 2006; here's one

from EurActiv, a news service covering the EU: http://www.euractiv.com/en/trade/wto-panel-rules-eu-gmo-moratorium-illegal/article-152341

14) Two interesting analyses of the meaning of the WTO's decision come from the Congressional Research Service's "Agricultural Biotechnology: The U.S.-EU Dispute," a report to Congress on March 10, 2006; and from Friends of the Earth International, "Looking behind the U.S. spin: WTO ruling does not prevent countries from banning GMO's," February, 2006.

15) Forty-nine of sixty major European retailers contacted by Greenpeace in 2005 said they would not sell food containing genetically modified ingredients in their stores, "EU Markets Report," Greenpeace International, February 3, 2005

16) "Directive 2004/35/CE of the European Parliament and of the Council, of 21 April, 2004, on environmental liability with regard to the prevention and remedying of environmental damage," otherwise known as the Liability Directive.

17) Interview with Frederique Lorenzi, European Commission, Brussels, July 1, 2005.

18) http://www.foeeurope.org/press/2007/May30_HH_EU_US_docs.htm

19) "Countries of Destination and Commodities Exported, 1996-2005," USDA, Economic Research Service.

20) "World Agricultural Supply and Demand Estimates," Economic Research Service, USDA, December 9, 2005.

21) Telephone interview with Dan McGuire, in Lincoln, NE March 27, 2007.

22) Telephone interview with Arnaud Apoteken, in Paris, March 21, 2006.

23) Telephone interview with Larry Keene, in Bloomington, IL, March 14, 2006.

24) Telephone interview with Mark Kimbale, in Newark, DE, December 17, 2006.

25) Firm Blames Farmers, 'Act of God' for Rice Contamination, Rick Weiss, *Washington Post*, November 22, 2005; "GM Rice: Standing Committee backs Commission Decision on strict counter testing of U.S. rice imports," press release by European Commission, Brussels, October 23, 2006.

Chapter 6

1) *Electronic Waste: Strengthening the Role of the Federal Government in Encouraging Recycling and Reuse*, Government Accountability Office, November, 2005, # GAO-06-47.

2) E-Waste, the hidden side of IT equipment's manufacturing and use, *Environment Alert Bulletin*, United Nations Environment Program, January 2005.

3) Electronic Waste and eCycling, Environmental Protection Agency. www.epa.gov/region1/solidwaste/electronic/index.html

4) *Exporting Harm: The High-Tech Trashing of Asia*, February 2002, and *The Digital Dump: Exporting Use and Reuse to Africa*, October 2005, both by Basel Action Network.

5) "Toxic Tech: Pulling the Plug on Toxic Electronics," Greenpeace International, May 2005.

6) *High Tech Trash: Digital Devices, Hidden Toxics and Human Health*, Elizabeth Grossman, Island Press, 2006.

7) BAN compilation of ratifications: http://ban.org/country_status/country_status_chart.html

8) WEEE Directive http://eurlex.europa.eu/LexUriServ/LexUriServ.do?uri=CELEX:32002L0096:EN:HTML

9) Interview with Rosalinde van der Vlies, Environment Directorate, Brussels, June 24, 2004.

10) Telephone interview with Mike Wallace, in San Francisco, CA, September 7, 2006.

11) *Electronic Waste: Strengthening the Role of the Federal Government in Encouraging Recycling and Reuse*, Government Accountability Office, November, 2005, # GAO-06-47.

12) Telephone interview with Barbara Pyle by my research intern Samuel Schramski, May 1, 2006.
13) Frequently asked questions on Directive 2002/95/EC on the Restriction of the Use of Certain Hazardous Substances in Electrical and Electronic Equipment (RoHS) and Directive 2002/96/EC on Waste Electrical and Electronic Equipment (WEEE), DG Environment.
14) "U.S. Technology Exports Up by $8 Billion in 2005," News Release from the American Electrical Association (AEA), April 19, 2006.
15) Interview with Michael Kirschner, in San Francisco, CA, June 9, 2006.
16) Electronics, Unleaded, Niall McKay at Center for Investigative Reporting, *The Economist*, March 10, 2005.
17) Interview with Craig Hillman, in Santa Clara, CA, February 9, 2006.
18) Apple to halt sale of some products to Europe, Katie Marsal, *Apple Insider*, June 21, 2006.
19) "Treo breaches RoHS directive, Palm left red-faced," Nancy Gohring, pcadvisor.co.uk, July 4, 2006.
20) The Electronics Industries Alliance maintains a comprehensive data base, EIA Track, of global chemical and recycling laws impacting the electronics industry: http://www.eiatrack.org/
21) Telephone interview with Rick Goss, in Washington, DC, September 1, 2006.
22) Telephone interview with Richard Ritchie, in Fairfield, NJ, August 23, 2006.
23) End of Life Vehicles Directive: http://europa.eu.int/eur-lex/pri/en/oj/dat/2000/l_269/l_26920001021en00340042.pdf
24) Telephone interview with Mike Taubitz, in Pontiac, MI, May 5, 2006.
25) Telephone interview with Mike Taubitz, in Pontiac, MI, May 16, 2006.
26) Global Automotive Declarable Substance List (GADSL), ver. 3.0, 2007.
27) Telephone interview with David Hutton, in Hampshire, England, October 16, 2006.
28) Telephone interview with Martha Bucknell, Sacramento, CA, with my researcher Samuel Schramski, May 5, 2006.

Chapter 7
1) Interview with Karl Wagner, in European Parliament, Brussels, October 6, 2005.
2) *Generations X: Results of WWF's European Family Biomonitoring Survey*, October 2005. http://assets.panda.org/downloads/generationsx.pdf
3) Interview with Kalliopi Vogiatzi, in the European Parliament, Brussels, October 6, 2005.
4) Interview with Eleonora Bruno, in the European Parliament, Brussels, October 6, 2005.
5) E-mail from Eleonora Bruno, May 8, 2006.
6) Telephone interview with Donatella Caserta, in Rome, May 16, 2006.
7) Levels of Risk: Common Industrial Chemicals in Tiny Doses Raise Health Issue, Peter Waldman, *Wall Street Journal*, July 25, 2001.
8) Fertile Ground for Inquiry: Environmental Effects on Human Reproduction, Julia R. Barrett, *Environmental Health Perspectives*, vol. 114, no. 11, November, 2006. http://www.ehponline.org/members/2006/114-11/EHP114pa644PDF.PDF]
9) Third National Report on Human Exposure to Environmental Chemicals, Centers for Disease Control and Prevention, 2005. http://www.cdc.gov/exposurereport/pdf/thirdreport.pdf
10) "Body Burden—The Pollution in Newborns," Environmental Working Group, July 14, 2005. http://www.ewg.org/reports/bodyburden2
11) "A Present for Life," Greenpeace UK, September 8, 2005. http://www.greenpeace.org/international/press/reports/umbilicalcordreport

12) "Pollution in People: A Study of Toxic Chemicals in Washingtonians," Toxic Free Legacy Coalition. http://www.pollutioninpeople.org/
13) http://www.pbs.org/tradesecrets/
14) *Trading Up: Consumer and Environmental Regulation in a Global Economy*, David Vogel, Harvard University Press, 1997, pp: 79-82.
15) *Green Chemistry in California: A Framework for Leadership in Chemicals Policy and Innovation*, Michael P. Wilson, with Daniel A. Chia and Bryan C. Ehlers, prepared for the California Senate Environmental Quality Committee and the California Assembly Committee on Environmental Safety and Toxic Materials by the California Policy Research Center at UC Berkeley, 2006.
16) "Chemical Regulation: Approaches in the United States, Canada, and the European Union," report by the Government Accountability Office for Senators Patrick Leahy, Frank Lautenberg and James Jeffords, November 4, 2005, pg. 2.
17) "Overview: Office of Pollution Prevention and Toxics Programs," report by EPA, January 2007, pp. 7-8.
18) *Chemical Regulation: Options Exist to Improve EPA's Ability to Assess Health Risks and Manage Its Chemical Review Program*, Government Accountability Office, (GAO-05-458), June, 2005.
19) "Asbestos Statistics," U.S. Geological Survey, last updated April 10, 2006.
20) Interview with Joseph Guth, Berkeley, CA, July 20, 2006.
21) *Globalization and Its Discontents*, Joseph Stiglitz, W.W. Norton, 2002.
22) Telephone interview with Malcolm Woolf, in Washington, DC, March 1, 2006.
23) "Chemical and Related Manufacturing: Top Contributors to Federal Candidates and Parties," Center for Responsive Politics. http://www.opensecrets.org/
24) Telephone interview with Lynn Goldman, John Hopkins University, February 13, 2007.
25) Telephone interview with Robert Donkers, in Washington, DC, July 16, 2004.
26) Interview with Andrew Fasey, in Santa Clara, CA, during a REACH training session sponsored by the Lowell Center for Sustainable Production for firms in the Silicon Valley, September 13, 2006.
27) Interview with Robert Donkers, in Berkeley, CA, March 17, 2006.
28) Interview with Bo Manderup Jensen, in European Parliament, Brussels, June 9, 2004.
29) European Chemical Industry Council (CEFIC), "Facts and Figures." http://www.cefic.org/factsandfigures/
30) Interview with Nicolas Thery, in Brussels, July 12, 2005.
31) Interview with Robert Donkers, in Brussels, June 30, 2005.
32) Telephone interview with Charlotte Brody, in Washington, DC, September 14, 2004.
33) Telephone interview with Stacy Vandeveer, in Providence, RI, January 22, 2007.
34) "Roundtable on Transatlantic Standards Issues: Meeting Notes," U.S. Department of State, January 10, 2005.
35) http://www.corporateeurope.org/
36) Interview with Anja Duchuteau, in Brussels, October 11, 2005.
37) Telephone interview with Joe Mayhew, in Washington, DC, November 9, 2004.
38) U.S. Representative Henry Waxman launched an investigation into the Bush administration's lobbying against REACH and released a report with his findings: "A Special Interest Case Study: The Chemical Industry, the Bush Administration, and European Efforts to Regulate Chemicals." The report, released on April 1, 2004, includes many internal administration cables and position papers that shaped early U.S. opposition to the European's efforts. The trip to Greece is mentioned in cable traffic from the U.S. Embassy in Athens to the State Department in Washington, on March 12, 2003. The cable's subject heading is: EU Chemicals Regulation: Industry Representatives Strategize on Engaging the Greek Presidency. It reads, in part: "Dow Chemical executives representing industry concerns about new EU chemicals regulations visited

Greece to discuss how to engage the Greek government in its role as EU president to influence draft legislation governing the regulations."

39) "Comments of the United States on Notification G/TBT/N/EEC/52 Regarding European Commission Regulation COM(2003) 644," a complaint by the United States to the WTO's Technical Barriers to Trade Committee on REACH, submitted June 21, 2004.

40) "Response from the European Communities to Comments Submitted by WTO Members Under G/TBT/N/EEC/52 (Regulation Concerning the Registration, Evaluation and Authorization of Chemicals, Known as REACH)," submitted to the Technical Barriers to Trade Committee on October 28, 2004; also, "The History of REACH," a Power Point presentation by the European Commission.

41) Interview with Cristina Travagliati, in European Parliament, Brussels, October 11, 2005.

42) Telephone interview with Tiffany Harrington, in Arlington, VA, February 1, 2007.

43) Interview with Peter Schmitt, in European Parliament, Brussels, October 11, 2005.

44) E-mail from Charles Auer, September 19, 2006.

45) www.courtinginfluence.net

46) Two Old Foes Plot Tactics in Battle over Judgeships: Neas and Gray Shape a Clash Growing More Vitriolic as November Vote Nears, *Wall Street Journal*, March 2, 2004; and, Chamber of Commerce Targets State Races: Money Pours Into Ads Challenging Candidates who are seen as Anti-Business, *Wall Street Journal*, September 16, 2004.

47) Interview with Susan Danger, in Brussels, October 18, 2005.

48) Telephone interview with Daryl Ditz, in Washington, DC, July 14, 2006.

49) Telephone interview with C. Boyden Gray, in Washington, DC, September 26, 2006.

50) "EU Trading Partners Call for Further Improvements to REACH," Press Release from U.S. Mission to the European Union, June 9, 2006, with track changes indicating it was written the previous day at AmCham EU.

51) E-mail from U.S. Mission to the European Union to more than three dozen MEP's, with subject heading: "REACH Second Reading: US Views," October 9, 2006.

52) Telephone interview with a confidential source, November 13, 2006.

53) http://reach.jrc.it/docs/reach_regulation/reach_corrigenda_june07.pdf

54) E-mail from Eleonora Bruno, January 28, 2007.

55) Telephone interview with Malcolm Woolf, in Washington, DC, June 13, 2006.

56) Interview with Mike Wilson, in Berkeley, CA, February 12, 2007.

Chapter 8

1) Stacy Vandeveer interview, in Providence, RI, January 22, 2007.

2) "Implications of REACH for the Developing Countries," by Frank Ackerman and a team of researchers at the Global Development and Environment Institute, Tufts University, in collaboration with the International Chemical Secretariat in Sweden. The study was commissioned by DG-External Policies and submitted to the European Parliament in March, 2006.

3) "Global Chemicals: China Remakes an Industry," *McKinsey & Co Quarterly*, Special Report 2004.

4) The Faces of Chinese Power, David M. Lampton, *Foreign Affairs*, January/February 2007, pg. 121. A similar figure is cited in the book, *Fast Boat to China: Lessons from Shanghai—Corporate Flight and the Consequences of Free Trade*, Andrew Ross, Pantheon Books, 2006, pg. 62.

5) "China: Air, Land and Water: Environmental Priorities for a New Millennium," World Bank, 2001.

6) "Scorched Earth: Will Environmental Risks in China Overwhelm its Opportunities?" Elizabeth Economy and Kenneth Lieberthal, *Harvard Business Review*, June 2007, pg. 90.

NOTES

7) Telephone interview with Tseming Yang, at Vermont Law School, South Royalton, VT, August, 23, 2006.

8) Telephone interview with C Boyden Gray, Washington, DC, September 26, 2006.

9) For details on China's RoHS, see the explanation by the American Electrical Association: http://www.aeanet.org/GovernmentAffairs/gabl_ChinaRoHSpage0905.asp
Other explanations of China RoHS include: "China RoHS Scope Clarified," Michael Kirschner, Green Supply Line, March 27, 2006; and "Environmental Alert: China. English Translation of Frequently Asked Questions on China's Measures for the Administration of the Control of Pollution by Electronic Information Products," briefing series paper published by the international law firm Wilmer Cutler Pickering Hale and Dorr, July 2006.

10) Exporting Harm: The High-Tech Trashing of Asia, February 2002, and The Digital Dump: Exporting Use and ReUse to Africa, October 2005, both by Basel Action Network.

11) Confidential interview with an electronics industry source, April 18, 2006.

12) Interview with Michael Kirschner, San Francisco, March 1, 2006.

13) "U.S. Technology Exports Up by $8 billion in 2005." American Electronics Association (AeA) release, (includes export-import statistics), April 19, 2006.

14) Telephone interview with Lynn Goldman, Johns Hopkins University, February 13, 2007.

15) Interview with Qi Ye, in Berkeley, CA, April 28, 2006.

16) China Urges Chemical Exporters Well Prepared for REACH," Xinhua News Service, December 20, 2006.

17) Telephone interview with Magnus Gislev, in Beijing, January 15, 2007.

18) Interview with Nicolas Thery, in Brussels, July 12, 2005.

19) Telephone interview with Orville Schell, Berkeley, CA, June 3, 2006.

20) Interview with C. S. Kiang, in Berkeley, CA, February 13, 2007.

21) Telephone interview with Michael Wolfe, Oakland, CA., August 28, 2006; and 'Companies Dump Toxic Goods on U.S. Consumers," Marla Cone, *Los Angeles Times*, October 16, 2006.

22) The PRC's Evolving Standards System: Institutions and Strategy, Chaoyi Zhao and John M. Graham, *Asia Policy Journal*, no. 2, July 2006, pp. 63-87.

23) Telephone interview with Gary Schmitt, spokesperson for the NREL, with my research intern, Emma Brown, May 18, 2007.

24) Telephone interview with Jeff Logan, in Washington, DC, February 26, 2007.

25) *The World*, broadcast on public radio, December 15, 2006, correspondent Mary Kay Magistad.

26) Telephone interview with Mark Levine, in Berkeley, CA, April 28, 2006.

27) Letter from John Bruton, EU Ambassador to the United States, to U.S. Senator Barbara Boxer, February 22, 2007.

28) Figures provided by Magnus Gislev, EU Environmental Counselor to China.

29) Telephone interview with Yingling Liu, in Washington, DC, January 8, 2007.

30) *Taming American Power: The Global Response to U.S. Primacy*, Stephen M. Walt, W. W. Norton & Co, 2005.

31) *State and Trends of the Carbon Market 2006: A Focus on Africa*, Karan Capoor, Sustainable Development Department, World Bank, November, 2006.

32) Telephone interview with Daryl Ditz, in Washington, April 13, 2007.

Chapter 9

1) Telephone interview with Stacy Vandeveer, in Providence, RI, January 22, 2007.

2) "View of US's global role 'worse'," BBC News, January 23, 2007. http://newsvote.bbc.co.uk/mpapps/pagetools/print/news.bbc.co.uk/2/hi/americas/6286755.stm

3) Corporate European Observatory in Amsterdam tracks—and helps to unearth—conflicts of interest inside the European Commission. www.corporateeurope.org
   Also, Brussels Special Advisers to Be Named, Andrew Bounds, *Financial Times*, February 18, 2007.

4) "Could Try Harder: A midterm report on the European Commission's environmental record," an assessment by the Green 10, a coalition of leading environmental NGO's operating throughout the EU. http://www.eeb.org/activities/General/g10_midterm_complete.pdf

5) Telephone interview with Robert Donkers, in Washington, DC, April 11, 2007.

6) Europe Is Giving Global Economy a Surprise Boost Amid U.S. Lull, Marcus Walker, *Wall Street Journal*, December 6, 2006; U.S. Economy Heading for Soft Landing, *Investment Week News*, March 9, 2007.

7) *A New World Order*, Anne-Marie Slaughter, Princeton University Press, 2005, pg. 63.

8) Interview with David Wirth, at Vermont Law School, South Royalton, VT, July 22, 2004; also the implications of 'Cassis' are described in *Trading Up: Consumer and Environmental Regulation in a Global Economy*, by David Vogel, Harvard University Press, 1997, pp: 29-33.

9) Interview with Camilo Barcia-Garcia, in San Francisco, October 14, 2004.

10) Interview with Penelope Naas, in Washington, DC, September 21, 2006.

11) Telephone interview with John Warner, in Lowell, MA, Septermber 11, 2006.

12) *Green Chemistry in California: A Framework for Leadership in Chemicals Policy and Innovation*, Michael P. Wilson, with Daniel A Chia and Bryan C. Ehlers, prepared by UC Berkeley California Policy Research Center for the state Senate Environmental Quality Committee and Assembly Committee on Environmental Safety and Toxic Materials, 2006, pg. 44.

13) Interview with Mike Wilson, in Berkeley, CA, February 12, 2007.

14) Interview with Michael Kirschner, in San Francisco, March 13, 2007.

15) "REACH Seminar on New EU Chemical Regulations," Department of Commerce, BuyUSA program, Charlotte, North Carolina, February 27, 2007.

16) "Maintaining Global Readiness in a Dynamic Regulatory Environment," workshop co-sponsored by the Toxics Use Reduction Institute, University of Massachusetts, Lowell, for the Department of Defense procurement division and defense contractors in Monterey, California, February 20-23, 2007.

17) Telephone interview with Adam Schafer, in Washington, DC, by my researcher Samuel Schramski, February 27, 2006.

18) Telephone interview with David Wirth, in Boston, MA, December 13, 2006.

INDEX

ACKNOWLEDGMENTS

I would like to thank the Center for Investigative Reporting, which for thirty years has supported independent journalistic endeavors like this one. My CIR colleagues, past and present, showed great patience and commitment: Dan Noyes, Christa Scharfenberg, Burt Glass, and Robert Rosenthal. I would like to thank Judy Alexander, long-time CIR board member and attorney who provided an important legal reading of the text. Samuel Schramski came to CIR as a sharp young intern and provided invaluable research on the book in its early stage before heading off to graduate school, as did Emma Brown in its later stage. And I would like to acknowledge the specific contribution to this book made by David Weir—who thirty years ago showed inexplicable faith in me as a young reporter and brought me into a project that later became the book *Circle of Poison*. That book was written at a time when the U.S. held a position of environmental leadership, and its subject was the hypocrisy with which, from that perch, it then treated the citizens of other nations. Now, the U.S. is on another end of that dynamic as the historic tables have turned, and so, in many ways, this book is a sequel.

A book is built over the years from editors who offer those ingredients that are critical to the life of a writer: trust and space. I'd like to express my appreciation to Victor Navasky, who in the 1980s was possessed with the wild idea of sending me to Paris for *The Nation*—enabling me to make many visits to Brussels and begin reporting on the evolving European Union from the inside. Since then, years later, his successors Katrina van den Heuvel and Betsy Reed stood behind an untested idea that enabled me to pursue an article that ultimately led to this book. Alison Humes at *Condé Nast Traveler* also has long seen the interesting interface between politics and travel, and enabled me to make a return trip to Brussels, that "hot" European capital. I would also like to thank Bill Moyers, who sent me, a writer, off with a camera crew to cover a story that appears in greatly expanded form in this book, and who, in addition to providing an inspiring example of journalistic integrity, wrote to me the memorable words, "Remember, some of the best sentences in the English language are short." I've recalled that advice frequently, though I have not, alas, always adhered to it.

My friend Mark Hertsgaard was generous with his comments and critiques of early drafts as the book evolved, as were Mark Dowie and Phillip Frazer, who provided valuable commentaries on various components of the book. Thanks to Peter Cunningham for whom riffing is an art form, and others who listened to my riffs and who played a role in sustaining this book without perhaps even knowing it: Safir Ahmed, Kevin Berger, Beau Friedlander, Gary Kamiya, Pamela Meyer, Louise Rubacky, Jon Marc Seimon, David Shearer, David Talbot, Sandy Tolan, and Tim

Trompeter; and to friends in Brussels and elsewhere—Frederique Lorenzi, Dan Bilefsky, Brigitte Alfter, Juliane von Reppert Bismarck—all of whom helped me navigate in one form or another that foreign capital; and Istvan Hegedus, whose contribution was to invite me to speak at Central European University in Budapest and get me thinking about this topic. And to many others who, were I to list, would last at least another chapter. I would also like to express my gratitude to the Vermont Law School, which awarded me a fellowship to study in those exalted quarters the intersection of trade, law, the environment, and human health—wherein lie the hidden powers elaborated on in this book.

I'm sure I'm not the first to discover that writing a book requires not only stamina but solitude. My deep appreciation to Gordon Knox for providing me with a refuge at the Montalvo Arts Center in Saratoga, CA; to Chris Desser, who carved out space for me in her office under the shadows of the Golden Gate Bridge; and to the San Francisco Writers Grotto, where I had the pleasure to be stationed for some months in the company of other writers with obsessions equal to my own.

Nor can a book be built on sheer energy alone. Financial support was provided by the Fred Gellert Foundation, the Wallace Global Fund, the Deer Creek Foundation, the Mitchell Kapor Foundation, the Overbrook Foundation, As You Sow, and by the Institute of Governmental Studies Center on Institutions and Governance at UC Berkeley. Heddy Riss, the Institute's program director, provided a great sounding-board for ideas, friendship and a biting Belgian humor over the course of this project. Many thanks to all for their support and affirmation—and to Peggy Lauer, whose enthusiasm for this project was contagious.

Ultimately, from the idea to the screen to the page, it was the crack team at Chelsea Green who played a key role in bringing this project to fruition: Thanks to Margo Baldwin, John Barstow, Emily Foote, Jonathan Teller-Elsberg and the rest of those mischievous Vermonters.

Finally, nothing would have been possible without my family—brothers Seth and Erik, whose family bias of support never flagged; and Abby Asher Schapiro and my niece and nephew Shayna and Avi—who sacrificed a part of his summer to learn about journalism and helped acquaint me with some of the inner workings in our state capitol before heading off to Georgetown University. My cousin Stephen Kamelgarn, M.D., provided me some valuable orientation to the human metabolism and its interactions with toxic chemicals. My French cousin Daniel Kamelgarn and his family provided a hideout in Paris, and Daniel shared with me his expertise on the EU, where he worked for several years. And last, but by no means least, my wife Deborah, who endured several years of what seemed one long endless deadline and provided that combustible mix along the way of love and editorial advice.

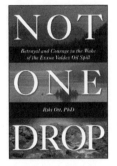

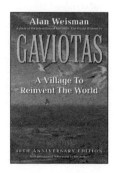

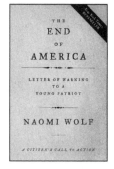